Download the New In Chess app:

- get early access to every issue
- follow every move on the built-in board

Read New In Chess on your tablet, smartphone or Windows PC, two weeks before the printed edition lands on your doormat, and replay all the moves in the interactive chess viewer

You can now download the digital edition of New In Chess on your tablet, phone or PC/notebook and read all the stories immediately after publication. By simply tapping on the games you can replay the moves on the interactive chessviewer. So from now on you don't need a board and set to fully enjoy what top grand-masters have to say about their games! The New In Chess app installs in seconds, has all the right features and is easy to operate. We have made an entire issue available as a FREE DOWNLOAD.

The chess magazine that moves
Now available for iOS, Android and Windows

NEW FRITZTRAINER DVDs

Let Nick Pert demonstrate a sharp new weapon for your repertoire: The Kalashnikov Sicilian!

Become a London System practitioner with Simon Williams' new DVDs.

Or get on the Queen's Indian train with a great new DVD by Sergei Tiviakov!

SIMON WILLIAMS: THE LONDON SYSTEM WITH 2.Bf4 RELOADED

Over the last couple of years nearly all the world's elite grandmasters have been employing the London System, and on this DVD Simon Williams shows what we can learn from their practice. The "Ginger GM" takes a look at all the latest developments whilst teaching you all the basics that you need to know in order to play this opening with success. Following his first bestseller on the London System, Williams' new work not only updates previous analyses but is also packed with new and original ideas which can be used even at the highest level. If you're not a practitioner of the London System yet, in fact the only question remains: "Why Not?"

29,90 €

SIMON WILLIAMS: TACTIC TOOLBOX LONDON SYSTEM

Let Simon Williams show you all the complications in the London System one has to know as White, giving you the tactical tools for a successful practice – the player who knows the typical motifs has an advantage over the board. Using the interactive FritzTrainer format which invites the viewer to answer questions by entering the moves on the screen Williams intensively and systematically makes your familiar with a multitude of typical tactical finesses.

29,90 €

SERGEI TIVIAKOV: QUEEN'S INDIAN DEFENCE – THE MODERN APPROACH

Sergei Tiviakov presents a complete repertoire for Black with the Queen's Indian Defence. The grandmaster explains everything one needs to know after 1.d4 Nf6 2.c4 e6 3.Nf3 b6, more profoundly, extensively and thoroughly than ever before. Of the total running time of more than 9 hours, 6 hours alone are dedicated to White's most popular continuation 4.g3. The material of the single chapters is based mostly on the author's own games and his life-long experience with the QID. Attached to this DVD, there is an exclusive collection of Sergei Tiviakov's complete games with the Queen's Indian Defence and a compilation of selected annotated games.

29,90 €

NICHOLAS PERT: A SICILIAN STUNNER – THE KALASHNIKOV

The Kalashnikov is closely related to the Sveshnikov but with much less theory to learn. This increasingly popular opening is easy to pick up as the Black pieces can usually be developed quickly and smoothly. The starting position for this video series is 1. e4 c5 2. Nf3 Nc6 3. d4 cxd4 4. Nxd4 e5. Pert: "When I was looking for a Sicilian variation to play, this one ticked all of the boxes. Many of the ideas are thematic and Black can achieve attacking positions in several of the variations. The lines have all been thoroughly checked and will hopefully provide the viewer with the confidence to play this opening."

29,90 €

ChessBase GmbH · News: en.chessbase.com · CB Shop: shop.chessbase.com
CHESSBASE DEALER: NEW IN CHESS · P.O. Box 1093 · NL-1810 KB Alkmaar
phone (+31)72 5127137 · fax (+31)72 5158234 · WWW.NEWINCHESS.COM

'I prefer learning from my own mistakes.'

CONTRIBUTORS TO THIS ISSUE
Simen Agdestein, Vladimir Barsky, Maxim Dlugy, Anish Giri, Dommaraju Gukesh, John Henderson, Dylan McClain, Ian Nepomniachtchi, Peter Heine Nielsen, Maxim Notkin, Arthur van de Oudeweetering, Judit Polgar, Alejandro Ramirez, Matthew Sadler, V. Saravanan, Wesley So, Jan Timman, Jonathan Tisdall

Delivering Chess

Thanks to the Internet, you can have anything delivered to you. The takeaway delivery industry has been revolutionized with bike-riding couriers taking food right to your doorstep. Now in Russia, they are doing the same for chess — only with couriers on horseback!

DeliveryChess (deliverychess.ru) was created as a PR campaign for SKB Kontur, the title sponsor for the Eurasia Open International Chess Festival that took place in early August in the Russian Urals city of Ekaterinburg. The month-long campaign in the run-up to the tournament — which was opened by 12th World Champion Anatoly Karpov — saw couriers attired in checkered suits, on horseback, delivering chess sets to residents across the city.

The chess sets were guaranteed to be delivered within 30 minutes, and the campaign proved to be a big hit, receiving hundreds of requests to deliver chess sets to homes and offices in the first couple of days after the service launched. It also looks set to be extended, as city officials announced that Ekaterinburg would be bidding to host the 2020 Candidates Tournament. ∎

Inside Chess

It is a scene we've seen captured many times by photographers and replicated in the movies: prison inmates playing chess against each other, whether it be through the bars of the cell or perhaps even in the exercise yard.

But now prisoners are representing their country at chess in international

American inmates representing their country as they compete internationally. Online, of course.

competition, and over multiple continents. And for obvious reasons they had to do so online.

In early August, the first International Online Chess Tournament for Prisoners, under the auspices of FIDE, pitted inmates from seven countries against each other.

Anatoly Karpov made the ceremonial opening address via a live video link and awarded special prizes. After some fierce competition, where, er, no prisoners were taken, hot favourites Russia – who only recently held a tournament with 21,000 inmates taking part – took the title. Belarus and Italy tied for second place, Armenia came in fourth, the United States fifth, Brazil sixth and England seventh.

The inspiration behind the event was Karpov and Dr. Mikhail Korenman, the Russian emigré academic who is also his long-time associate and who set up a pioneering chess program for inmates inside Cook County Jail in Chicago.

Their work has been applauded

and closely observed by the Department of Corrections (DOC). 'This is not just another activity in our jail... This sport is transformative,' Cook County Sheriff Tom Dart commented. 'Patience, planning ahead and learning to be less impulsive are some of the benefits of playing chess,' he added.

Korenman also noted that a study in Brazil found that chess-playing prisoners were less likely than others to return to incarceration, an advantage he said could be related to the game. 'It teaches them a different way of thinking,' he said. 'That's my guess. In a real-life situation, they can predict what will happen if they do something.'

Whatever did happen to...

Over the years, *The Onion* has garnered a reputation as being America's best-known satirical newspaper. Normally, they would take a mainstream political story and turn it into something so silly, so ridiculous, that, momentarily, you could be forgiven for thinking it just could be for real, realize it isn't, and just laugh.

The mocked-up photo of Deep Blue spending its days unrecognized in Washington Square Park.

However, in today's politics they face formidable challenges as anything could be real.

But when you can't rely on politics, then there's always chess – and one Onion story that brought tears to our eyes was the revelation that it had uncovered the sad plight of IBM's

Deep Blue, with a wonderful mocked-up photo about how it had hit hard times in retirement, and reduced to hanging out all day unrecognized at the public chess tables in Washington Square Park in New York.

'Deep Blue used to be a legend,' said park regular Natalie Bryant. 'Today, hardly anyone wants to play with it, and not because of its brute-force, quasi-artificial-intelligence approach to the game. It's just a sad, old, washed-up box to these kids.' Other Washington Square Park regulars said the retired computer 'seems completely fine' with simply entering sleep mode and spending its cold, lonely nights on a park bench.

Decades Apart

Despite going a little more grey on top, some players continue to impress with their longevity in the game. Mickey Adams, for example, whom we congratulate after winning his seventh British Championship title in Torquay over the summer. Undefeated on 7½/9, not only did Adams take the first prize of £5,000, but he also had the personal satisfaction of edging out his nearest rival, David Howell, who replaced him as the new England No.1, and now seems set to reclaim his longtime top spot in the ratings.

Here's how Adams beat IM Richard Pert (twin brother of GM Nicholas Pert!) in an attractive attacking game that brought him the sole lead.

Adams-R.Pert
Torquay 2019
position after 28.. ♖a7

Mickey Adams was rightly pleased with his 7th British title in thirty years.

29.♕g5! Taking full advantage of the back-rank mate. **29...♕d8 30.♕h4!** Like some sort of medieval torturer, Adams is very adept at ruthlessly stretching opponents in such positions. **30...♔e8 31.♗xe7** Black resigned. There's no answer to 31...♖axe7 32.♕h8+ ♖f8 33.♕xg7!.

Adams' latest victory comes in the 30th anniversary of his first British championship win back in 1989 at the age of 17 – a British age record he still holds today. The span between these victories led many to speculate whether this, too, could be a world record?

Far from it, it seems. For many years, Sammy Reshevsky held the record with 33 years between his first (1936) and the last (1969) of his eight US titles. Others also had victories decades apart, with New Zealand legend Ortvin Sarapu 38 years between his first (1952) and last (1990) national titles and Max Euwe 34 years between his first (1921) and last (1955) victories in the Netherlands.

These are the three top established gaps – as far as we're led to believe – between first and last national title victories. Does anyone know any different? If so, we'll be only too glad to hear from you.

The secret of his success

How often have chess players been caught in a toilet, as they were trying to cheat with the help of their smartphone? Too often, and you'd love to think that at some point nobody would be stupid enough to try it again – but obviously not!

The latest GM 'flushed with success' is Igors Rausis, who at 58 is the oldest among the world's top 100 grandmasters. Over the past few years he had steadily risen to No. 52 with an Elo of 2685. At an age when a player should be haemorrhaging Elo points, the Latvian/Czech actually gained some 200 points. Many wanted to know the secret of his success, but others had become suspicious about Rausis' rise and had already placed him on a 'watch list'.

Thanks to another smartphone function of taking photos – sneakily taken by a private and unidentified individual not connected to the tournament – the grandmaster was caught red-handed using a smartphone in a toilet cubicle to analyse one of his games during the Strasbourg Open in France. A remorseful Rausis later told the Czech newspaper *Lidovky*: 'I signed a statement that I am guilty in full ... I completely ruined my name and also destroyed the trust of all my colleagues and friends.'

Rausis is now suspended, with his case set to go before the FIDE ethics committee, and he's resigned to the fact that he'll likely be stripped of his title. There's talk that his wrongdoing has also been reported to the French police.

The fateful photo of Igors Rausis as he is caught red-handed in a French toilet.

Knight Rider

Just where the hell are all those flying cars we were promised as kids? They're still not here yet, so instead we may have to make do for now with cars that can play chess. Yes, you heard right: cars that play chess.

The Tesla electric car company started pushing out a new 'Arcade' app for its in-car infotainment system back in late June at the annual E3 gaming conference. The highlight of the software update was the somewhat bewildering hoopla announcement that the car can now play humans at chess.

that looks like a good move to me so he's so hitting my bishop

A Tesla that plays chess? Self-driving sounds challenging enough.

But Elon Musk likely didn't imagine that his innovative car company was designing a chess program that would immediately be challenged by one of the world's best players! A couple of days after the launch, a video appeared on YouTube of Fabiano Caruana taking on the Tesla Model 3. But Deep Blue versus Kasparov, this was not. The car made some questionable moves and was crushed in 21 moves and in under five minutes. Caruana gives it a little credit at the end of the video, diplomatically calling the game 'challenging'. In the car's defence, it was stationary, with the engine not running – we think the odds go up significantly for the car when it hits 70 mph on the freeway! ∎

NEW IN CHESS bestsellers

The Hippopotamus Defence
A Deceptively Dangerous Universal Chess Opening System for Black
Alessio De Santis   320 pages - €29.95

"Little short of a revelation. De Santis really has come at his subject from all conceivable angles to leave no stone unturned. Did you know that the hippopotamus is the most dangerous of all large animals? In chess opening terms, I would argue that it's also the case." – GM Glenn Flear

"Presents a very good view on the many ideas that the Hippopotamus offers." – IM Dirk Schuh

An Attacking Repertoire for White with 1.d4
Ambitious Ideas and Powerful Weapons
Victor Moskalenko   368 pages - €29.95

"Crammed full of opening ideas which will suit players of all strengths. His mix of wit, weapons and wisdom strikes me as the ideal source for anyone seeking inspiration."
GM Glenn Flear

"A host of interesting new and dangerous ideas."
John Upham, British Chess News

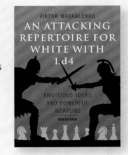

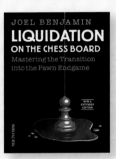

Liquidation on the Chess Board – New and Extended Edition
Mastering the Transition into the Pawn Ending
Joel Benjamin   304 pages - €27.95

"An excellent guide to a difficult theme that has been badly served in chess literature."
IM Frank Zeller, Magazine Schach

"Benjamin tackles one of the most important (and underappreciated) aspects of endgame practice."
GM Daniel Naroditsky, Chess Life Magazine

Winning Ugly in Chess
Playing Badly is No Excuse for Losing
Cyrus Lakdawala   336 pages - €22.95

When was the last time you won a perfect game? Lakdawala demonstrates the fine art of gaining undeserved victories by refusing to resign in lost positions, throwing vile cheapos, provoking unforced errors and other ways to land on your feet after a roller-coaster ride. If you rather win a bad game than lose a good one, this is your ideal guide.

Bobby Fischer Comes Home
The Final Years in Iceland, a Saga of Friendship and Lost Illusions
Helgi Olafsson   144 pages - €19.95

"A personal and heartbreaking account. Destined to be a classic." – *John D. Warth, ChessCafe*

"A fascinating read, in turns poignant and perplexing, and I recommend it wholeheartedly to anyone interested in the second Pride and Sorrow of American Chess."
Ken Surratt, ChessVille

The Longest Game
The Five Kasparov-Karpov Matches for the World Chess Championship
Jan Timman   304 pages - €29.95

"The ultimate book on Karpov-Kasparov. Jan Timman has again written a monumental history book."
Johan Hut, Noord Hollands Dagblad

"There is something extremely satisfying about reading about events that you know well, and then discovering that you've forgotten or never noticed some important details!"
Grandmaster Matthew Sadler

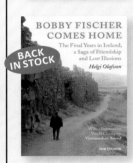

The Power of Pawns
Chess Structures Fundamentals for Post-Beginners
Jörg Hickl   192 pages - €18.95

"The didactic concept of the book is admirable. Each chapter defines the structures, explains the typical characteristics and shows the plans for both White and Black. The reader invariably receives useful tips for practical play."
Harry Schaack, KARL magazine

"There are lots of valuable training lessons, in particular in areas where chess engines offer no help."
Harald Fietz, SchachMagazin 64

Strategic Chess Exercises
Find the Right Way to Outplay Your Opponent
Emmanuel Bricard   224 pages - €24.95

Finally an exercises book that is not about tactics!

"Bricard is clearly a very gifted trainer. He selected a superb range of positions and explains the solutions extremely well." – *Grandmaster Daniel King*

"For chess coaches this book is nothing short of phenomenal." – *Carsten Hansen, author of The Full English Opening*

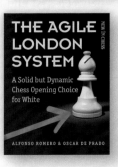

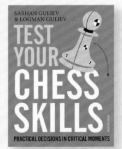

Test Your Chess Skills
Practical Decisions in Critical Moments
Sarhan & Logman Guliev   180 pages - €19.95

"The best book in this genre that I have seen in recent times. The reader has to face the same problems as during a real game. Working diligently with this entertaining work will improve the performance of a wide range of club players. Above all their strategic and analytical skills."
Uwe Bekemann, German Correspondence Chess Federation

The Agile London System
A Solid but Dynamic Chess Opening Choice for White
Alfonso Romero & Oscar de Prado   336 pages - €26.95

Reveals the secrets behind sharp ideas such as the Barry Attack, the Jobava Attack and the hyper-aggressive Pereyra Attack.

"With plenty of fresh material that should ensure that it will be the reference work on the complete London System for years to come." – *GM Glenn Flear*

"Encyclopedic in scope." – *John Hartmann, ChessLife*

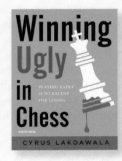

Superiority

I was puzzled when reading Judit Polgar's column in New In Chess 2019/5 to see her group together Alekhine, Fischer, Karpov and Kasparov as examples of champions who demonstrated their superiority not only in matches but also in tournaments. To group Fischer with the three, who more than any of the others (before Carlsen) dominated tournament play while they were champions, seems a gross injustice. A remarkable talent, undeniable, great results prior to becoming champion, no argument, but as World Champion – as we all know – Fischer did not win as much as a single game of chess either in tournament or match play. That is not the way to demonstrate superiority.

Markus Lømo
Fredrikstad, Norway

Just checking

In New In Chess 2019/5 you asked GM Romain 'Who is your favourite chess player of all time?' I laughed out loud upon reading his reply. He did equivocate when, after answering 'Magnus Carlsen', by saying, 'I believe it's the first time we have a World Champion who is better than all his contemporaries in all aspects of the game.'

The GM needs a history lesson. Surely he has heard of Bobby Fischer, a player who was lightyears ahead of every other human player on earth at every form of chess played when he was playing. Then there was Paul Morphy, who was certainly far above every other chess player living at the time 'in all aspects of the game.'

Michael Bacon
Lavonia, GA, USA

Disturbing picture

While I enjoy your magazine I have to comment on the terrible photo of Ian Nepomniachtchi that defaces the cover of New In Chess 2019/5. I have never seen such an angry expression of a chess player captured by a photographer. I wonder what the photographer did to generate such wrath?

I find the picture so disturbing that I have to leave the magazine turned over so that it is hidden. Both Nepo and your readers deserve better.

Dave Broughton
Port Hope, Canada

Write to us
New In Chess, P.O. Box 1093
1810 KB Alkmaar, The Netherlands
or e-mail: editors@newinchess.com
Letters may be edited or abridged

Only victories

In reaction to the experiment with the Armageddon Norway Chess format (see New In Chess 2019/5): another idea to reduce the number of draws could be to count only the victories. It would be nice to once try this format in a tournament too. Just analyse several crosstables and you will easily see the differences.

Nol van 't Riet,
Gouda, The Netherlands

Falklands/Malvinas (1)

Writing about the Islas Malvinas/Falkland Islands, Nigel Short looks at the conflict exclusively from the British viewpoint, while so many died on both sides because of the British attack. Former Prime Minister Margaret Thatcher spoke about 'aggressors'. How many times in its history has the United Kingdom – once the greatest colonial power – been the aggressor?

A FIDE-Vice President should not write exclusively from one point of view.

Martin Dissertori
Appiano-Eppan, Italy

Falklands/Malvinas (2)

The readers of your prestigious magazine have been able to read in New In Chess 2019/5 GM Nigel Short's views about the Malvinas-Falkland chess affair. Evidently he presents a partial vision, as member of the ECF, that ignores resolutions of the UN and the International Olympic Committee and is deprived of impartiality.

I believe that you should also give the President of the Argentine Chess Federation, Mario Petrucci, the opportunity to give his version and to share his vision of this chess tournament held in the islands, that sought to unite people under the motto 'Gens Una Sumus'.

Arturo Alvarez
Rosario, Argentina

Falklands/Malvinas (3)

Thinking that I was a subscriber to a chess magazine, I was unpleasantly surprised by the article of Nigel Short in New In Chess 2019/5. Was he writing as a FIDE Vice-President or just as someone from the U.K.? It was an uninteresting article about a totally insignificant event in one of the remnants of the famous British Empire, made mighty by God, as they are still singing over there. The photo of Short at Falkland Home settled it for me. A waste of pages.

Bab Wilders
Amersfoort, The Netherlands

COLOPHON

PUBLISHER: Allard Hoogland
EDITOR-IN-CHIEF:
Dirk Jan ten Geuzendam
HONORARY EDITOR: Jan Timman
CONTRIBUTING EDITOR: Anish Giri
EDITORS: Peter Boel, René Olthof
PRODUCTION: Joop de Groot
TRANSLATORS: Ken Neat, Piet Verhagen
SALES AND ADVERTISING: Remmelt Otten

PHOTOS AND ILLUSTRATIONS IN THIS ISSUE:
Cook County Jail/DOC, Frederic Friedel,
Lennart Ootes, Niki Riga, V. Saravanan,
John Upham, Berend Vonk

COVER PHOTO: V. Saravanan

© No part of this magazine may be reproduced, stored in a retrieval system or transmitted in any form or by any means, recording or otherwise, without the prior permission of the publisher.

NEW IN CHESS
P.O. BOX 1093
1810 KB ALKMAAR
THE NETHERLANDS

PHONE: 00-31-(0)72-51 27 137
SUBSCRIPTIONS: nic@newinchess.com
EDITORS: editors@newinchess.com
ADVERTISING: otten@newinchess.com

WWW.NEWINCHESS.COM

Magnus on the March, in Perspective

Magnus Carlsen has been the top-ranked player for more than a decade and World Champion since 2013, so it is not news that he is the best player in the world. But this year, he has been on a tear, winning tournament after tournament and going undefeated against the best of the rest of the world. His streak is quite impressive, but he still has a way to go if he is to surpass the all-time benchmarks for consecutive tournament victories and longest unbeaten streak, as the following charts show. *DYLAN LOEB McCLAIN*

Most classical, or slow, games played in world-class competitions without a loss*

Ding Liren
100 games
August 2017 - November 2018

The strongest Chinese player to date, Ding's streak was part of his rise to a rating of over 2,800. He is currently ranked No. 3 in the world.

Mikhail Tal
95 games
October 1973 - October 1974

Though the former World Champion was known for a highly risky style of play, particularly early in his career, during the early 1970s he played far more positionally.

Mikhail Tal
86 games
July 1972 - April 1973

Tal enjoyed a resurgence in the early 1970s that would take him to the No. 2 ranking in July 1973.

Vladimir Kramnik
82 games
January 1999 - July 2000

The streak was just before his title match against Garry Kasparov -- a match in which he went undefeated to win the title. Given how solid Kramnik was, his presence on this list is not a surprise.

Wang Yue
82 games
March 2008 - December 2008

He has faded a bit in recent years and been eclipsed by younger players, so it can be easy to forget that he was once seen as China's great hope.

Magnus Carlsen
79 games
July 2018 - Present

His last loss was to Shakhriyar Mamedyarov in the Accentus Grandmaster Tournament in Switzerland.

Wesley So
67 games
July 2016 - April 2017

During the streak, he won the Sinquefield Cup, London Classic and Tata Steel tournaments and also went undefeated in the Chess Olympiad.

Maxime Vachier-Lagrave
67 games
October 2015 - September 2016

By the end of the streak, he was ranked No. 2 in the world and had a career-high rating of 2819.

José Raúl Capablanca
63 games
1916 - 1924

Capablanca won the World Championship during the streak (a 14-game match against Emanuel Lasker).

* This list excludes the performances of three players who had long unbeaten streaks, but whose games were not always against the world's best. Those players are Sergei Tiviakov, who went 110 games without defeat during 2004 to 2005 (though he did play Vasily Ivanchuk, Teimour Radjabov, Levon Aronian, and Carlsen during that period); Bogdan Lalic, who also went undefeated over 110 games, from June 2006 to March 2007, and 101 games in 2008; and Milan Drasko, who had a streak of 84 games from October 2006 to September 2007.

Most consecutive elite tournaments won (includes ties and rapid and blitz, which have become popular formats in recent decades)

Garry Kasparov
15 tournaments

U.S.S.R. Champ. 1981	Optiebeurs, Amsterdam 1988
Bugojno, Bosnia 1982	GMA, Belfort 1988
Moscow Interzonal 1982	U.S.S.R. Champ. 1988
Niksic, Montenegro 1983	GMA, Reykjavik 1988
OHRA, Brussels 1986	GMA, Barcelona 1989
S.W.I.F.T. Brussels 1987	GMA, Skelleftea 1989
Tilburg, Netherlands 1989	
Belgrade Investbank 1989	
Linares, Spain 1990	

Alexander Alekhine
10 tournaments

Kecskemet, Hungary 1927	London 1932
Bradley Beach 1929	Pasadena 1932
San Remo, Italy 1930	Mexico City 1932
Bled, Slovenia 1931	Paris 1933
Bern, Switzerland 1932	
Bern, Swiss Champ. 1932	

Anatoly Karpov
9 tournaments

Tilburg 1977	Bugojno 1980
Bugojno, Bosnia 1978	Amsterdam 1980
Montreal 1979	Tilburg 1980
Waddinxveen, Netherlands 1979	
Tilburg 1979	
Bad Kissingen, Germany 1980	

Carlsen
8 tournaments

Sinquefield Cup 2018	Norway 2019
World Blitz, Russia 2018	Grand Chess Tour, Zagreb 2019
Tata Steel, Netherlands 2019	
Shamkir, Azerbaijan 2019	
Grenke Classic 2019	
Grand Chess Tour Côte d'Ivoire 2019	

Fair & Square

Hunter Davies: 'In the chess world they can't decide whether chess is a sport, a game or an art. After 24 hours in their company, I'd say chess is a drug. They are all addicts, players and press.' *(The British author and only authorised biographer of the Beatles, profiling Nigel Short for The Independent newspaper during his 1993 Candidates Final against Jan Timman)*

Daniil Kharms: 'When two people play chess, I am always under the impression that one is fooling the other. Especially if they play for money.' *(The mid-1930s Soviet avant-gardist absurdist poet and writer)*

Daniil Dubov: 'Whenever I see chess, I start to feel better.' *(The World Rapid Champion in a Eurosport '24 Hours with...' video profile)*

Henrikh Mkhitaryan: 'I play football like chess. You have to think a lot and anticipate what could happen after you make your move. If you make a mistake, your opponent can punish and you end up losing the game.' *(Arsenal's talismanic midfield play-maker)*

Boris Johnson: 'Chess is a fantastic game, it teaches rules and discipline, it is a very logical game, it directs the energy of children in a certain direction, otherwise they might start making mischief, it makes sense to encourage them to deal with chess, it's the biggest puzzle game ever invented.' *(The new British Prime Minister, in 2014, when he was Mayor of London, at the London Chess Classic)*

Robert Grudin: 'Chess, which exists predominantly in two dimensions, is one of the world's most difficult games. Three-dimensional chess is an invitation to insanity. But human relationships, even of the simplest order, are like a kind of four-dimensional chess, a game whose pieces and positions change subtly and inexorably between moves, whose players stare dumbly while their powerful positions deteriorate into hopeless predicaments and while improbable combinations suddenly become inevitable. To make matters worse, some games are open to any number of players, and all sides are expected to win.' *(The American writer and philosopher, in his 1982 book 'Time and the Art of Living')*

Demis Hassabis: 'The reason that I could not become a professional chess player is that it didn't feel productive enough somehow.' *(The former England leading junior player and now DeepMind CEO, interviewed in the August edition of Wired magazine)*

Bent Larsen: 'I don't care very much for miniatures. I don't try to beat my opponents quickly because if they are strong, I think I should respect them. It is too risky to play sharply to beat them in 20 moves.'

Alexander Grischuk: 'Maybe classical chess can be compared to the Tour de France, because it's very boring and goes on for days.' *(During the Rapid and Blitz Paris Grand Chess Tour)*

Malcolm Gladwell: 'There are no instant experts in chess – certainly no instant masters or grandmasters. There appears not to be on record any case (including Bobby Fischer) where a person reached grandmaster level with less than about a decade's intense preoccupation with the game. We would estimate, very roughly, that a master has spent perhaps 10,000 to 50,000 hours staring at chess positions...' *(The chess-loving Canadian journalist and author of the best-seller 'Outliers' in 'The New Yorker' magazine in August 2013)*

Wayne Xiong: 'Coaching is very important. Sometimes parents want to do too much by themselves. This is a professional job. You may be a great engineer, a great scientist. But you are not a great chess coach. Being a chess coach takes experience.' *(The father of leading US junior GM Jefferey Xiong, speaking to US Chess Online during the World Open in Philadelphia)*

Paul Morphy: 'The ability to play chess is the sign of a gentleman. The ability to play chess well is the sign of a wasted life.'

Classic Magnus
World Champion unstoppable in Zagreb

Public interest for the chess grandmasters in Zagreb was heart-warming and it was no secret who was everyone's favourite.

In another sparkling show of creativity and willpower, Magnus Carlsen continued his winning streak, outclassing the field in the first classical leg of the Grand Chess Tour. **ALEJANDRO RAMIREZ** watched the World Champion's chess with pleasure and wonders whether the Norwegian is nearing his theoretical maximum or poised to cross new frontiers.

LENNART OOTES

C hess form at elite level is a finicky thing. Many factors have to come together for a super-GM to perform at top level – study must be kept up, the player must be in the right state of mind, health issues should be minimal... the list goes on and on. To play at the very best of your capacity, game after game, for months and months, seems a hercu-

lean task. Somehow, Magnus Carlsen and his team have either figured it out or have been blessed with all the circumstances aligning, because it is clear that the World Champion is not only winning tournament after tournament, but doing so considerably ahead of his competitors.

The Grand Chess Tour is an important part of the chess calendar now, the strongest circuit in the world. Even before the start of the first leg of the 2019 tour, the Rapid and Blitz in Abidjan, there was little doubt

that Carlsen would be among the top contenders, with possibly the only question remaining how dominant he would be. Rapid and blitz have always favoured the Norwegian, and his form after convincingly winning Wijk aan Zee, Shamkir and the Grenke Classic showed that his classical chess was coming back to that mythical 2014 level. Magnus half-joked during the World Championship match against Caruana that Carlsen 2014 would be his favourite player from the past. This might change soon.

The GOATs of chess
The intrepid format of this year's Norway Chess allowed for different interpretations by the puritans of classical chess of how the tournament really went. Carlsen 'only' scored +2 in the classical games, but won the tournament with a round to spare, dominating every Armageddon he played in, except against Caruana. His form in Zagreb, in the first classical leg of the 2019 Grand Chess Tour, however, cannot be contended – it was exceptional, impressive, and a final nail into the coffin of nay-sayers to the argument that he is a mandatory inclusion in the list of the GOATs of chess, along with Kasparov and Fischer.

Carlsen's first game in Zagreb followed the style he has dazzled us with since the beginning of the year. Uncompromising, strategically risky chess in which material and structure can be shed for the power of initiative and attack. Anish Giri was unable to cope with the problems, something the World Champion might have foreseen. '...d6 was a case of playing the man and not the position... d6 is such a stupid move he wouldn't have looked at it.' This is what Carlsen told commentator Maurice Ashley about his decision to shatter his pawn struc-

It is clear that the World Champion is considerably ahead of his competitors.

ture and get a dangerous position. Giri was clearly not up to the job, and after making some questionable decisions he was simply getting mated.

NOTES BY
Alejandro Ramirez

Anish Giri
Magnus Carlsen
Zagreb 2019 (1)
Sicilian Defence, Rossolimo Variation

1.e4 c5 2.♘f3 ♘c6 3.♗b5 e6
A bit of a deviation. 3...g6 was the main topic of the first half of the World Championship, before Caruana switched to 3.d4.
4.♗xc6 bxc6 5.d3 ♘e7 6.h4 h5 7.e5

[chess diagram]

Anish Giri shares a joke with Garry Kasparov. His game against Magnus Carlsen turned into a cold shower as the World Champion successfully wrong-footed him with his risky opening choice.

16.♘e2?
A very clumsy move. The knight going to d4 was not such a big threat as to warrant White wasting time to prevent it, certainly not with an already developed piece.
16.♗e3 ♖c8 17.♕b7 keeps the game complicated.
16...♖c8 17.♕a4
To me, this was the final mistake. A computer might hold it after this, but it was clear that Giri was not really aware of where the ball was rolling. The queen is completely misplaced on the queenside.
17.♕e4 ♘d6!? 18.♕d3 h4 looks nice for Black, but the game goes on.

17...♖c7!
A lovely manoeuvre. Carlsen utilizes his pieces in a surprising but excellent way.
18.♗f4 ♖d7

19.c3
The spoil-sport computer says that 19.♘g3 gives White plenty of hope, but even here 19...♘h4 is quite unpleasant.
19...g5 20.♖ad1?!
20.♗e5 f6 21.♗h2 h4 looks very ugly.
20...♖xd1 21.♖xd1

7...d6 7...f6 is more or less the normal break, keeping the central structure intact. Surely, Giri had some idea here, but we might never know what it was.
8.exd6 ♘g6 9.♘fd2 Played after a very long think. This may be a bit more precise than 9.♘bd2 (although I don't think so), but from a practical point of view it was easier to develop normally.
9...♗xd6 10.♘c4 ♗e7 11.♘c3 ♗a6

12.♕f3?! The start of a strange idea. 12.♗d2! was the only way to keep an advantage, simply not caring about the h4-pawn: 12...♗xc4 13.dxc4 ♘xh4 (13...♕d4 14.♕e2 ♘xh4 15.g3 ♘f5 16.0-0-0 seems very dangerous for Black, who can't really castle in any direction after taking on h4)

14.g3, and White recovers the pawn on h5.
12...♗xc4

13.♕xc6+ White gets c6, but it's not a great pawn. And h4 will not be saved. **13...♔f8 14.dxc4 ♘xh4 15.0-0** Castling into the storm a bit, but still not a mistake.
15...♘f5

21...♛a8! Giri had flat-out missed this idea. The queen on a8 does a superb job of attacking the kingside, and it cannot be opposed. White's position simply collapses.
22.♗c7 h4 23.f3 h3
White resigned.

It is easy to get lost in only covering Carlsen's performance in this event, but the first round of Zagreb was one of the most epic ones in recent history, rivalling that first round of the 2015 Sinquefield Cup. Fabiano Caruana came up with a nice, home-cooked idea against Hikaru Nakamura's predictable Queen's Gambit system, and the U.S. Champion was unable to navigate the treacherous complica-

tions on his own. Wesley So outplayed Ding Liren from an equal position, and the Chinese player made things worse by blundering in an already difficult situation. So turned out to be a revelation in this tournament, but we will get to that later. Ian Nepomniachtchi had a blistering start, even though his chess was questionable at many points, including his first round win against Vishy Anand. Despite finding some good resources, it was clear that his opening play had left him in some trouble; but he turned things around and won.

The tournament was off to a great start, and then things started to cool down a bit, at least in terms of decisive results. In the second round, the three 2800s of the event (Carlsen, Caruana, Ding Liren) had their opponents under immense pressure. Carlsen got into a superior endgame against Anand and was clearly outplaying his opponent, Caruana's recent adoption of the Sveshnikov gave him an overwhelming position against Nepomniachtchi, and Ding Liren's excellent exchange sacrifice had Karjakin's position in ruins. Yet even these three

aren't immune to mistakes, and in a surprising twist of events Carlsen was unable to convert a technical win, Caruana's time-pressure and over-zealousness cost him a point, and Ding Liren never found the coup de grâce. Nepomniachtchi emerged as the early leader, but with a questionable game in Round 1 and being against the ropes on Round 2, it was hard to say he was a favourite to win the tournament in such a long event.

We had it, at last!
Shakhriyar Mamedyarov is a player that brings wonderful imagination to the game, but sometimes he creates some really awful games, and that is what he did against Nepomniachtchi in Round 3, simply collapsing out of the opening with the white pieces and allowing his opponent to finish off the game in whichever way he pleased.

**Shakhriyar Mamedyarov
Ian Nepomniachtchi**
Zagreb 2019 (3)

position after 26...h4

Black's position looks so good that at the first glance you'd think that a serious sacrifice must have been made to achieve such promising control of e4 and kingside possibilities, not to mention that basically dead bishop on b2. But, no, it was just a pawn.
27.♘e5 Desperate. **27...h3!?**
27...dxe5 28.dxe5 ♘e4, and Black has no reason to believe that he has given up any compensation by taking the piece. But Nepomniachtchi wasn't interested in material just yet.

After three rounds Ian Nepomniachtchi was a full point ahead of Magnus Carlsen, but in the end the Russian finished 2½ points behind his Norwegian friend.

28.♘xg4 ♘xg4 29.gxh3 ♘xe3 30.♖c3 ♘f5

White's king is simply too exposed.
31.♖d1 ♛h5 32.♖f3 ♗h6
White resigned.

After three rounds, we had it, at last! Someone was a full point ahead of Carlsen in a tournament! Could we finally be talking about someone else winning an event? Would the Russian star have his breakthrough moment? A point ahead, but as Kasparov pointed out, Nepomniachtchi had yet to play Carlsen himself, and Carlsen was clearly hungry for another first place.

The next round was difficult to explain. Some blamed the heat that was engulfing the Croatian city, some the loud playing conditions. Some players pointed out that they were tired after a long series of events, which included the Grand Prix Series and Norway, others just shrugged their shoulders and said 'Well, that's chess'.

Nepomniachtchi was clearly worse against Karjakin after only 10 moves as White, but as if lacking the killer instinct, the former World Championship Challenger simply traded the queens into a drawn endgame instead of really pushing Nepomniachtchi's position. Karjakin's form in Zagreb was simply bad, and he let go of a few half points that should have been his.

Carlsen-Mamedyarov was an entertaining affair. Out of the opening, Mamedyarov was simply

busted. White got everything he could dream of with a strong pawn centre and an open h-file against the Grünfeld, and Carlsen had two choices of how to convert: the slow but methodical 12.♗d3 or the powerful 12.♘g5, which required precision and accurate calculation. True to his new style, he chose the attacking option, but he misplayed it badly and suddenly found himself in trouble. The game was tense, with Mamedyarov playing for a win for most of it, but Carlsen managed to hold on to that half point. To top it off, MVL and Giri suffered from a shared case of blindness.

Maxime Vachier-Lagrave
Anish Giri
Zagreb 2019 (4)

position after 33.♛xd5

After outplaying his opponent, Giri has become a bit over-aggressive and has been losing the thread of the game. His next move is a big blunder.
33...♘g5? 33...♖8g6 keeps some compensation, and the game is quite murky.
34.♘xf4?? 34.♖xf4 ♖xh3+ 35.gxh3 ♛xh3+ 36.♔g1 looks extremely dangerous for White, but there is no effective check for Black. 'You're not surprised that there is a checkmate here for Black, so you don't question it if you see one,' was the way MVL justified the double oversight.
Here 36...♘f3+ 37.♔f2 ♖g2+ 38.♔e3 ♘g1+ 39.♖1f3 ♖xe2+ 40.♔d3 is just one example of the king escaping, which MVL pointed out he had missed from afar.

34...♘xh3 35.♛xg8+ ♖xg8 36.♘xh3 ♛xd4 37.e6

The passed pawn on e6 gives about enough compensation to secure the draw.
37...♛d6+ 38.♘f4 ♖f8 39.g3 ♖xf4 40.gxf4 ♛xe6 41.f5 ♛h6+ 42.♔g3 ♛g5+ 43.♔h3 ♛h5+ 44.♔g3 ♛g5+ 45.♔h3 ♛h5+ 46.♔g3
Draw.

After a couple of rounds with few headlines came Round 6. The first game clearly heading for a decision was Ding Liren-Nepomniachtchi. After surviving some questionable positions in the event, Ding's handling of the English was simply exemplary, and with the Russian's king stuck in the middle there simply was no way that he would let go of his win. The Chinese player applied the finishing touches with confidence. Wesley So played a very fine game against Mamedyarov.

NOTES BY
Wesley So

Wesley So
Shakhriyar Mamedyarov
Zagreb 2019 (6)
English Opening, Marshall Gambit

Chess-wise, Croatia was a very inspiring country for me. I don't think we ever before had such intense and focused audiences. Usually when people come to the venue, they stay for a few moves, take their pictures and then hang out in the hallway chatting and watching the games on their phones, happy to let the engines do the thinking for them.

Not the Croatian fans. They lined up early and packed the hall to standing room only. Then they stayed for *hours* and watched every game, trying to work out the lines along with the players. Their intelligence was inspiring and I may have played better because of them. These are the kind of fans that I enjoy, because they enjoy the game and not afraid to think for themselves.

1.♘f3 ♞f6 2.c4 g6 3.♘c3 ♝g7
This was totally unexpected. A couple of rounds earlier Mamedyarov had played 3...d5. Since he does not play the King's Indian, I figured out that he was going to play Dubov's idea with 4.e4 e5. I spent a long time here trying to decide which line I should go for.

4.e4 e5

5.♘xe5
Taking on e5 is the only way to fight for an advantage. 5.d4 won't yield anything. Actually, I played against it as Black three years ago against Lenderman, and I equalized smoothly. In fact, that was the last time that line was played at such high level:
5.d4 exd4 6.♘xd4 0-0 7.♗e2 ♖e8 8.f3 c6 9.♗g5 ♛b6 10.♕d2 d5 11.cxd5 ♞xe4 12.♘xe4 cxd5 13.♗e3 dxe4 14.♘b5 ♛f6 15.♘c7 ♖d8 16.♗g5 ♖xd2 17.♗xf6 ♖c2, with equality (½-½, 72) in Lenderman-So, St. Louis 2016.

5...0-0 6.♘f3 ♖e8

Wesley So keeps urging online viewers to ignore engines and use their own brains. 'Watching chess would be exciting, instead of "boring", as many chat room "experts" claim.'

7.♗d3 In the end I just decided to make a simple move, which I had also looked at.
I spent a long time calculating 7.d3 d5 8.cxd5 ♘xd5 9.♗d2, which was actually the main line of what I had prepared, but I have no idea what is happening in this position. Is White better, or does Black have enough counterplay? 9...♗g4 (9...♕d6!? is another serious move, as is 9...c5!?)

10.♗e2 ♗xf3 11.gxf3 ♘b4 12.♗e3 ♘8c6 13.a3 ♘a6, and I remember that the engine gives a stable advantage for White here, for no real reason. After 14.h4 (14.♘b5!?) 14...♘d4 15.h5 ♘c5 16.hxg6 hxg6 the situation is not so clear.

7...♘xe4 Up to here, Mamedyarov was still blitzing his moves. He always likes to blitz his moves in the opening. I think he has good memory.
I remember that the main line I looked at was 7...d5 8.cxd5 ♞f5 9.0-0 ♘xe4 10.♘xe4 ♗xe4 11.♗xe4 ♖xe4 12.♕b3 ♘d7 13.d3, when I can fight for an advantage, although Black has compensation for the pawn.
7...b5 8.0-0 bxc4 9.♗xc4 ♘xe4 is also worth considering.

8.♗xe4 8.♘xe4 does not work because of 8...f5.
8...♗xc3 After 8...f5 I have 9.d3.

These are the kind of fans that I enjoy, because they enjoy the game and are not afraid to think for themselves.

9.dxc3 ♖xe4+ 10.♗e3

10...d6 More accurate for Black here is 10...♘c6!. Now 11.c5 is met by 11...b6, so White goes 11.0-0 d6, and here c5 can simply be recaptured because the queen is defended. After 12.♕d2 the position is close to equal, but I imagine everybody would prefer White, given the choice.
10...♖xc4 11.♕d5 leaves his rook at a difficult spot: after 11...♖a4 he wants to go ...♖a6, but 12.♘g5 should give me a huge attack.
11.c5 Because of his move-order now I get this extra option.
11...d5

12.h3 Preventing ...♗g4, but after the game I noticed that ♕d2 is even more accurate.
Best for me is 12.♕d2, when I have a large advantage. My knight can jump to d4 in one go, and I even get the option of castling queenside: 12...b6 13.0-0-0 c6 14.h4, and White is far better.
My first intention was 12.♘d2, but then I didn't want to allow 12...♖xe3+ 13.fxe3 ♕h4+ 14.g3 ♕h3, when I have many weaknesses, but in fact I should be able to consolidate with

♕f3 or ♕a4 (14...♕e7 is in fact stronger than 14...♕h3, when White only has a slight advantage, so in retrospect I was right not to allow the exchange sacrifice).
12...b6 13.0-0 ♗b7

14.♖e1
After 14.♘d2 I was concerned about the exchange sacrifice 14...♖xe3 15.fxe3 bxc5, but in fact it does not give Black enough, so he should simply withdraw his rook to e8 instead: 16.e4! dxe4 17.♘xe4 ♕xd1 18.♘f6+, and White wins.
14...♘d7 15.♘d2
Also possible is 15.b4, when White gets strong dark-square control for the doubled pawns. I didn't see a way to improve after 15...♕e7, but the computer suggests 16.♕d3 to meet 16...bxc5 with 17.♕b5.
15...♖e8
15...♖e6 is worth considering.
16.♘b3

16...♕h4
Here I realized I had to be careful with ...d4 ideas, freeing the b7-bishop from its tomb. My knight is quite far from the defence of my king. I have to watch out.

If 16...bxc5, I was simply going to recapture the pawn, 17.♗xc5 ♖xe1+ 18.♕xe1 a5 19.a4, and maintain enduring pressure.

17.♕d2 Fortunately, his ...d4 ideas do not work yet, and I have enough pieces to defend my king.

17...f6

17...♘e5 18.♗g5 ♕h5 19.f4 cuts Black's counterplay to pieces.

18.f4 I decided to make a practical decision and cut off his queen. This was what I was already planning when he played ...♕h4, so I just made the move relatively quickly. In fact, I have other tempting possibilities here as well:
– 18.♗d4 permanently cuts off his bishop from the long diagonal.
– 18.♗f4 is perhaps even stronger. The point is that after 18...♘e5 I have 19.♕d4, eyeing his queen, and after 19...♘d3 20.♕xd3 ♕xf4 21.♕b5 I consolidate and maintain a large endgame advantage: 21...c6 22.♕b4 ♕xb4 23.cxb4.

18...♕h5

18...f5 is worth considering, when he gets the e4-square permanently. Since 19.♗d4 is met by 19...♖e4, it is funny that the computer suggests 19.a4. Not so easy to find, but with a simple idea: to weaken his dark squares even more. 18...♖e4 loses to 19.♗f2 ♕xf4 20.♕xf4 ♖xf4 21.♖e7, when 21...♖d8 is met by the typical 22.c6! ♗xc6 23.♘d4 ♗b7 24.♘e6 ♖e4 25.♖e1.

19.♗f2

Here I was already looking at c6 ideas. The pawn sacrifice is already possible: 19.c6!? ♗xc6 20.♘d4 ♗b7 21.♘b5 d4 22.♘xc7! dxe3 23.♕xd7

♕h4 24.♕g4 ♕f2+ 25.♔h2, and White wins the exchange. I decided to wait one more move. But in fact 19.c6 is seriously worth considering. 19.a4, with the idea of a5, is also possible, when Black should sac a pawn with 19...d4 and 20...♕d5 to get some play on the long diagonal.

19...g5? This loses. For better or worse I thought that he had to go 19...d4 and hope to save the endgame a pawn down: 19...d4 20.♕xd4 ♘xc5 21.♘xc5 ♕xc5 22.♕xf6 (or 22.♕xc5 bxc5 23.♗xc5) 22...♖c6.
However, he had other alternatives. To begin with, 19...♔f7 looks logical to me. Black does not threaten anything; he just improves the position of his king.
19...♘f8 is the computer suggestion.

20.c6! A very strong move! Probably my best move in Croatia. In return for the pawn I get two tempi activating my knight and it disrupts the whole coordination of his pieces.
Normal moves do not give me anything particularly significant. If 20.♖xe8+ ♖xe8 21.♖e1 ♖xe1+ 22.♕xe1 ♕f7 I thought Black might just hold.

20...♗xc6 21.♘d4 ♗b7 22.♘b5 ♖xe1+ Desperation, but 22...♖ac8 offered a better defence.

After 22...♖ac8 23.♘xa7 ♖cd8 24.♘b5 ♖c8 both 25.a4 and 25.fxg5 ♕xg5 26.♕xg5+ fxg5 27.♗g3 give White a large advantage. I win a pawn in the final position.

23.♖xe1 ♖e8 24.♘xc7 ♖xe1+ 25.♕xe1

25...d4 Opening up the long diagonal, but a bit too late.

White would win with the same idea after 25...gxf4 26.♕e7 ♕f7 27.♕d8+ ♘f8 28.♘e8, when Black does not have an appropriate defence. 28...♘e6 is met by 29.♕b8! ♕f8 30.♘xf6+ ♔f7 31.♕xb7+ ♔xf6 32.♕xa7, and White snatches all his pawns.

26.♕e7! The final accurate move, sealing the win.

26.♗xd4 gxf4 27.♕e7 ♕g6 offers Black bigger chances of a successful defence, but White should still win the endgame after 28.♕d8+ ♘f8 29.♘d5 ♗xd5 30.♕xd5+ ♕f7 31.♕f5, although it's much more difficult.

26...♕f7

As I told the commentator after the

game, White is winning in all lines, but it is much harder than it looks to calculate it yourself without using three engines:

– 26...♕d1+ 27.♔h2 ♕f1 28.♕e6+! ♔h8 29.♕e8+ ♔g7 30.♕xd7+ ♔h6 31.fxg5+ ♔g6 32.♕e8+.

– 26...dxc3 27.♕xd7 cxb2 28.♕d8+! ♔g7 29.♘e6+ ♔g6 30.♕g8+ ♔f5 31.♘g7+, and it's mate.

The problem with following chess games live with computer engines is that it just shows the maths, without explaining why. It just gives +3 or +10, but it doesn't give any reasons. I believe people should start using their brains more when watching chess, instead of just looking at computer assessments without actually knowing where the pieces are. If they tried to think it out, watching chess would be exciting, instead of 'boring', as many chat room 'experts' claim.

27.♕d8+ ♘f8

27...♔g7 is much more tenacious, when I can just capture the pawn on d4 with my bishop, or calculate the forced win arising from 28.♘e8+ ♔h6 29.fxg5+ ♔g6! 30.♘d6! ♕e6, when White has a variety of wins, but, again, it's 10 times more difficult to see it without engine help.

28.♗xd4 gxf4 29.♘e8

29...♘e6

29...♕e6 threatens to mate me, but my attack comes first after 30.♘xf6+ ♔f7 31.♕c7+ ♕e7 32.♕xf4 ♘e6 33.♕f2 ♘xd4 34.♘d5+, and White wins.

Here Shakh decided to resign, while I was still calculating the position

after 30.♘xf6+ ♔g7 31.♘g4+ ♘xd4 (31...♔g6 32.♘e5+ forks his queen) 32.♕xd4+ ♔f8

ANALYSIS DIAGRAM

and in fact I didn't find a clear-cut way to win here, even though the computer gives the mathematical advantage of +4.00, so I should be able to win even if he played on.

Thank you to GM Zlatko Klaric of the Croatian Chess Federation for staging such an excellent and well-run tournament. Thank you to the wonderful Croatian chess fans who excited me with their dedication to the game of Kings.

■ ■ ■

The big divide

In the other games, almost as if to not be left behind, Caruana stepped out of his comfort zone a bit, playing the Arkhangelsk Variation in the Spanish against Maxime Vachier-Lagrave, who wasn't showing his best chess either in Zagreb. The American player dominated the game and emerged victorious in the complications. And there was more to come! Levon Aronian won a technical Berlin endgame against Karjakin, while Carlsen scored his 14th classical chess win against Nakamura.

It was clear now that the top half of the event was playing well, and the bottom half were simply not having a good event. A full point separated the players tied for 4th with 3½/6 and the rest of the field. Carlsen and So caught up with Nepomniachtchi to claim a share of the lead.

Back on top

There is always something powerfully psychological about the way your previous games in an event have gone. Playing badly gives you a slight sense of paranoia and inferiority, while playing well inspires you to keep trying your best and fighting for every half point. These feelings are sometimes exacerbated or fed on a free day, when your mind starts reflecting on what has happened so far.

Carlsen played another Sicilian, this time in a key game against Nepomniachtchi. A complex position, in which the traditional computers prefer White but never have a clear plan, resulted in the World Champion slowly outplaying his opponent. The Russian also seemed a bit lost, because his king was a permanent weakness in case the centre came unstuck. In a critical moment, Nepomniachtchi was faced with the following task:

As Sergey Karjakin is being told by Maurice Ashley what he has missed in his game against Wesley So, the American is finding out the same as he quickly checks the tactics on a laptop.

Ian Nepomniachtchi
Magnus Carlsen
Zagreb 2019 (7)

position after 27.♖ad1

27...f5 Played quickly, and despite it being based on an oversight, it's a good move.
28.gxf5? Nepomniachtchi didn't take as long for this move as one would have expected in such for crucial decision, but then again Nepo isn't the most patient player when it comes to time management.
After 28.exf5 ♗d4+ 29.♔g2 ♕e2+ 30.♔h1 (30.♔h3! was what Carlsen

had missed, when the king is surprisingly safe on h3) 30...♗f2 the World Champion felt that Black was winning, but White has a miraculous and unusual draw: 31.b4!, and there is no good way to defend against the perpetual of ♕a1+ and ♕a7+, which is quite surprising.
28...g4 The king is totally helpless in this line, and Black won quickly:
29.d4 ♕h4+

30.♔e2 ♕h2+ 31.♖f2 gxf3+
White resigned.

Carlsen was back where we have grown accustomed to seeing him: atop the leader-board, no questions asked. Not only that, but he

had also vanquished a traditionally tough opponent: this was Carlsen's first classical victory against Nepo. Second now was Wesley So on +2, and I think his survival of the following gaff can only be explained by the fact that Karjakin was no longer in the winning mindset.

Sergey Karjakin
Wesley So
Zagreb 2019 (7)

20.♖xe5 Karjakin has some pressure on the position with his rook on e5 and the somewhat exposed king.
20...♗d6??
A horrible blunder, but without thinking much Karjakin withdrew

his rook. White would have been slightly better after 20...♕d7 21.c3.
21.♖e2?? 21.♖xf5 did not cross the Russian's mind, and he quickly figured out that ...♗xh2+ wouldn't work when Maurice Ashley told him about the continuation: 21...♗xh2+ 22.♔h1 ♕h4 23.♖g5+ ♔h8 24.♖xg4

ANALYSIS DIAGRAM

and the queen cannot stay on the h-file due to the discovery.
21...♕f6 22.c3 ♖ae8 23.g3 dxc3 24.♗xc3 ♕f7 25.♖xe8 ♖xe8 26.♕d2 ♕e6 27.♕g5+ ♕g6 28.♕d2 ♕e6 29.♕g5+ ♕g6 30.♕d2 ♕e6 White resigned.

The Magnus train was not about to stop: Carlsen defeated another player he had never managed to beat, Ding Liren. His second Peter Heine Nielsen guides you through that one.

NOTES BY
Peter Heine Nielsen

Ding Liren
Magnus Carlsen
Zagreb 2019 (8)
Catalan Opening, Open Variation

1.d4 ♘f6 2.c4 e6 3.♘f3 d5 4.g3 ♗e7 5.♗g2 0-0 6.0-0 dxc4 7.♕c2

Ding shows his usual loyalty to his opening systems and plays his favourite line in the Catalan.
7...b5!?
Until a few years back, 7...a6 was considered mandatory, but now both 7...b6 and 7...c6, as well as the game move, have gained in popularity.
8.a4 b4 9.♘fd2!?
White's most critical move, intending to play a positional pawn sacrifice. Interestingly, Magnus's second

for the 2018 World Championship match, World Rapid Champion Daniil Dubov, tried 9.♘bd2 ♗b7 10.♘xc4 c5 11.dxc5 ♗e4 12.♕d2!?, gaining a slight endgame edge against Nakamura in the Moscow Grand Prix.
9...♘d5!?
This, however, is very rare, and stylistically very different from the main line 9....c6, when 10.♘xc4 ♕xd4 11.♖d1 c5 gives White good compensation for the pawn. Again, the recent action was from the Moscow Grand Prix, with Grischuk beating Nakamura as White.
10.♘xc4 c5 11.dxc5 ♗a6!

Technically, a novelty. Black used to take back on c5 in the few existing games with this line. Magnus afterwards admitted that this was preparation for the World Champion-

ship match, and it is indeed typical 'computer' chess, in which one pushes the position to its absolute maximum, relying on tactics.

12.♘e3 Ding, not having the comfort of having checked this position with a computer, faced a difficult task evaluating the numerous options. Many ideas look tempting for White, but as the assumption is that the World Champion does not play bad lines, he has to tread very carefully.

12.♖d1 is very logical, but after 12...♘d7 13.c6 ♖c8 14.♘e5 ♘xe5! Black has excellent counterplay.

12...♘d7 13.♘xd5 exd5 14.c6

14.♗xd5 ♖c8 15.c6 ♘e5 16.♖d1 transposes to the line below.

14...♖c8

A firm handshake seals Magnus Carlsen's first ever classical win against Ding Liren. A great show of strength by the champ, who showed his skills in all three phases of the game.

15.♗f4 Ding keeps finding good moves. 15.♖d1 ♘e5 16.♗xd5 ♘xc6! 17.♗xf7+ ♖xf7 18.♖xd8+ ♗xd8 is a strong queen sacrifice that yields excellent practical compensation. The computer says that White should try to force a draw straightaway in order not to be worse.

15...♘c5 16.c7 ♕d7 17.♘d2 g5!?

Continuing in modern computer

style and not caring for common sense chess like 17...♗d6 trying to round up the c7-pawn and restoring material equality, but again pushing the position to its limits.

18.♗e5 f6 19.♗d4 ♖xc7 20.♕d1

Carlsen later said that while he was obviously happy being in prep when his opponent was not, his position still did not inspire him with all that much

confidence. Objectively, Black is OK, but White's position is easier to play in view of Black's weakened king and numerous pawn structure defects. So Black has to keep exerting maximum pressure before White consolidates.

20...♘e6 21.♘b3 ♗c4!

An important move, disturbing White's plans just in time. If now 22.♗e3 then 22...d4! 23.♘xd4 ♘xd4 24.♗xd4 ♖d8

It is indeed typical 'computer' chess, in which one pushes the position to its absolute maximum, relying on tactics.

wins back the temporarily sacrificed pawn, with equality.

22.♘a5 ♘xd4 23.♕xd4 ♔g7!

A nice move, removing the king from the light squares so that, for example, ♗xd5 will never be a check now. But it's noteworthy that Magnus chooses the more active position on g7 instead of the seemingly safer place at h8. However, in the continuation of the game it is obvious that protecting f6 and being closer to the centre later on, are important factors.

24.♖fc1 ♗xe2 25.♖xc7 ♕xc7 26.♖e1 ♗c5 27.♕xd5 ♖e8

White has no way of exploiting the pin on the e-file and Ding has to start caring about safety. Here, however, he miscalculates. Now 28.♕c6! would be the correct way, the difference being that after 28...♕xc6 29.♘xc6 ♗h5, White has 30.♖c1!, when he will manage to liquidate the queenside and make a draw.

28.♕b7?! ♕xb7 29.♘xb7

29...♗f8 Now, however, things are different. As the game shows, Black has excellent chances due to the queenside targets he gets if the rooks are exchanged. So Magnus felt that 30.♘d8!? was by far White's best move, and while 30...♖xd8 31.♖xe2 ♖d1+ 32.♗f1 ♗c5 is still not exactly pleasant for White, he seems to be able to draw with accurate play, e.g. 33.♖e4 b3 34.♖c4 ♗d4 35.♖b4 ♖d2 36.♖xb3 ♗xf2+ 37.♔h1, when Black obviously has some initiative, but not enough for the win.

30.♗c6? ♖e7 31.f3 ♗c4 32.♖xe7+ ♗xe7

Black's advantage is obvious: the bishop pair and targets on both wings. Is it enough to win? I assume it is borderline, but to quote Bent Larsen: what matters practically is whether there are winning chances.

33.♔f2 f5 34.♔e3

34...♗g8!

A beautiful move, which even got praise in a tweet from Anish Giri. It exploits the entire board and thus exemplifies the difference between the knight and the bishop in mobility.

35.♔d3 g4!?

35...♗f6 is met by 36.♘d6, securing sufficient counterplay. Now, however, Magnus starts creating targets on the kingside, with ...h5 and ...h4 coming next. White's choice is which kind of fortress to go for. Playing f4 keeps the position closed, but risks the bishop landing on g1. fxg4, exchanging pawns, feels logical, but it leaves the black king a much easier path to White's camp via the centre. The right decision would actually have been to remain positive and push the a-pawn to a6, starting with 36.a5!. After 36...h5 37.a6, not only is the white pawn much closer to queening, forcing Black to be a bit more careful,

but it also leaves the b7-knight better protected. Black has several tries keeping practical chances, but objectively the position seems drawn.
36.♘a5 ♗c5

White's knight does get rerouted back to the defence, but at the huge price of allowing the bishop to penetrate to g1.
37.♘c4 ♗g1 38.♘e3 ♗e6 39.fxg4 fxg4 40.♔e2

Tactically White is OK, as after 40...♗xh2 41.♔f2 White threatens 42.♘f1, but Black will of course increase the pressure after forcing White into a completely passive position.
40...h5! 41.♗d5 ♗d7 42.♗b3 ♗xh2 43.♔f2 h4! 44.gxh4 ♗e5

In principle every exchange should get White closer to the draw, but the fact that Black has created a passed pawn is a much bigger factor.
45.♘c4 g3+ 46.♔g1 ♗f4 It's been a common quote of Magnus that he does not really believe in fortresses, a feeling that let him down in the fourth game of the World Championship match against Karjakin. But here everything is in order. Black's king will enter easily.
47.♗d1 ♗c6 48.b3 ♔h6 49.a5 ♗e4 50.♔f1 ♔g7 51.♔g1 ♔f6 52.♔f1 ♔e6 53.h5 ♔d5 54.a6 ♔d4 55.♗g4 ♔c3

56.♗e6 On 56.♗d1, 56...g2+ 57.♔g1 ♗d5 puts White in complete zugzwang.
56...♗c2 57.♘a5 ♗c7 58.♘b7 ♗d3+ 59.♔g1

59...♗xa6!? White resigned. My computer says 59...♗e4 is mate in seven, but criticizing a move that forces instant resignation is too much. An excellent game by Magnus, showing his skills in all three phases of the game.

■ ■ ■

That made it three in a row for Carlsen, two of them as Black. In the meantime, Wesley So took advantage of Nakamura's poor play in Zagreb. He outplayed his Olympic teammate with an interesting idea from the opening, but Nakamura fought back and was on the verge of saving the game when he sent his king the wrong way on move 36. Even then, at the very end, Nakamura could have made a draw, something that was shockingly missed by most of the chess media.

Wesley So
Hikaru Nakamura
Zagreb 2019 (8)

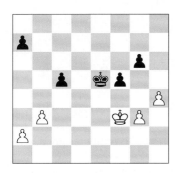

position after 47.b3

47...♚e6??
The right move was 47...a6!. Black can't give up space before weakening White's queenside first: 48.♚e3 a5 49.♚f3 (49.a4 ♚d5 50.♚d3 ♚e5 51.♚c4 ♚e4=) 49...♚d4 50.♚f4 a4!

ANALYSIS DIAGRAM

Kind of the point. This can be played here or on the next move, but it's more logical to do it now. 51.♚g5 ♚c3 (51...axb3 52.axb3 ♚c3 is the

Wesley So kept the pressure on Carlsen, but catching the World Champion proved to be impossible.

same) 52.♚xg6 axb3 53.axb3 ♚xb3 54.h5 c4 55.h6 c3 56.h7 c2 57.h8♕ c1♕, and even though Black will still have to suffer endlessly to save the half point, the table bases do say this is drawn.
47...a5 48.♚e3 ♚d5

ANALYSIS DIAGRAM

is one tempo short for Black. You can count them if you want.
48.♚f4 ♚f6 49.a3 a6 50.b4 c4 51.a4 ♚e6 52.♚e3 ♚d5 53.♚d2 ♚d4 54.♚c2 c3 55.b5
Black resigned.

With this win, So kept the pressure on Carlsen, but catching the World Champion proved to be impossible. It is good to see So back near the top of the standings, because since his tournament victories in 2016 he hasn't particularly shone in any event. It was also nice for the spectators, since there was still someone who could challenge Carlsen's lead, and the tournament wasn't simply over with several rounds to spare.

In that same Round 8, Anish Giri added to Mamedyarov's misery with a nice attacking game. The Dutchman had a poor start, but recovered with this game and a further win against Nepomniachtchi on the final day.

NOTES BY
Anish Giri

Anish Giri
Shakhriyar Mamedyarov
Zagreb 2019 (8)
Sicilian Defence, Rossolimo Variation

1.♘f3 c5 2.e4 ♘c6 3.♗b5
I had lost against Carlsen with the same Rossolimo in the first round, but I didn't think the third move was necessarily to blame for all my misfortunes in that game.
3...d6 Carlsen usually plays 3...g6 and 3...e6 in our game. Mamedyarov played the third option.
There are also rare moves like 3...e5!? or even 3...♕b6, by the way. Both were tried against me recently.
4.0-0 ♗d7 5.c3 ♘f6 6.♖e1 a6 7.♗f1 ♗g4

8.d4
The old main line is 8.h3, and there is nothing wrong with grabbing the bishop. But I wanted to try this more direct move, which has gained in popularity recently.
8...cxd4 9.cxd4 d5
The main move has been 9...e5, but what Shakh did shouldn't have ended that badly either.
10.exd5
I recalled the lines arising from here and they looked pretty nice for White, but it's possibly not the most ambitious approach.
10.e5 felt more critical, and then some e6/♖xe6 sacs was what I recalled, but I wasn't certain, so I decided to go for a small plus instead.
10...♘xd5

10...♗xf3 11.♕xf3 ♕xd5 also needs further investigation. Maybe Black can try to hold here too.

11.♘c3 e6 12.h3

12...♗h5? I was very happy to get to this position, as I remembered a Mickey Adams game in which he showed how White is supposed to play here. (Actually, I already realized during the game that the way that game proceeded was 8.h3 ♗h5 9.g4 ♗g6 10.d4 cxd4 11.cxd4 d5 12.exd5 ♘xd5 13.♘c3 e6 14.♘xd5.)

The alternative 12...♗xf3 13.♕xf3 ♗e7 14.♘xd5 ♕xd5 15.♕xd5 exd5 would have led to a very, very long game. White is of course better, but it wouldn't be easy to get anything real here, with Black having a very solid position in exchange for White's bishop pair.

13.g4! ♗g6 14.♘xd5 ♕xd5 15.♗g2

Suddenly Black is in trouble. His lag in development is not helping and ♘e5 is looming.

15...0-0-0

There were no fun options, but this is just really bad.

15...♗b4 16.♘e5 ♕b5 17.a4 ♕b6

Remembering a game of Mickey Adams, Anish Giri emerged from the opening with an overwhelming position. The rest was suffering for Shakhriyar Mamedyarov as White's hungry pieces descended on his poor king.

LENNART OOTES

18.♗d2 ♗xd2 19.♗xc6+ bxc6 20.♕xd2 is really bad for Black. He cannot castle in view of ♘d7+, and his c6-pawn will fall.

After 15...♗e4, 16.♖xe4 is a nice cheapo: 16...♕xe4 17.♘e5, and the queen is lost.

16.♘e5 16.♗g5 felt winning, too, but the game move is simple enough.

16...♕xd4 17.♕f3!

An important nuance, after which it is evident that Black is losing.

17...♖d5

Shakh tries to muddy the waters.

After 17...♕b4 18.♗f4 ♘xe5 19.♗xe5 ♗d6 I tried to find a forced win, but it was nice to know that even if I didn't

find it, I could just play 20.♗xg7 and win slowly. There are many ideas, e.g. ♖e3-♖b3, ♖d1-♖d4, etc. The material is equal but the difference in king safety seals the deal for White. Still, I assumed this was the best defensive attempt for Black.

18.♘xf7?!

Some move must be responsible for this game lasting so long, and I believe this was the one to blame, although the position remains totally winning.

18.♘xg6 is not necessarily better; just much simpler. Normally speaking, I would have played it, but when you haven't won any games for a while,

When you haven't won any games for a while, you assume that somehow it cannot be that simple.

you assume that somehow it cannot be that simple. After 18...fxg6 19.♗e3 ♕xb2 20.♕f7 it is really just game over.

18...♖g8 19.♘g5 ♗d6 20.♘xe6

20...♕b4 20...e5 is funky, but I can even walk into the trap: 21.♘xd4 ♖xe1+ 22.♗f1 ♘xd4 23.♕c3+ ♗c7 24.♕xd4 ♖d8 when, after 25.♕c4, White is nevertheless winning (25...♗d3 26.♕xc7+ ♔xc7 27.♗f4+).

21.♗e3

21.♗f4 ♖d3 22.♗xd6 ♕xd6 23.♖ad1 was a lazy way to do it.

21...♖e5 22.a3 For every queen move there is a good reply now. 22.♖ac1 wins as well, because after 22...♖xe6 23.♖xc6+ bxc6 24.♕xc6+ ♔d8 25.♗g5+ ♖f6 there is the strong 26.♗xf6+ (not 26.♖d1 ♔e7!) 26...gxf6 27.♖e6!, followed by ♕d5+ and ♖c6+, and then picking up the g8-rook in some lines.

22...♕xb2 After 22...♕c4 there

are two ways to win: 23.♘d4 ♗e4 24.♘xc6 ♗xf3 25.♘e5 ♗xe5 26.♖ac1, or 23.♖ac1!? ♕xe6 24.♖xc6+ bxc6 25.♕xc6+ ♗c7 26.♕b7+ ♔d8 27.♖c1. After 22...♕b3, 23.♘d4 is simplest: 23...♘xd4 24.♗xd4 ♖xe1+ 25.♖xe1 ♕xf3 26.♗xf3, and it will soon be more than just a pawn.

23.♖ac1!

Not a very sophisticated piece of calculation.

23...♖xe6 24.♖xc6+ ♔d7

24...bxc6 25.♕xc6+ is quite obviously lost.

25.♖xa6!? A little sadistic and lazy, but it does the job.

25.♖d1! bxc6 26.♕xc6+ ♔e7 27.♗g5+ ♔f8 28.♖xd6 would win easily, but you have to allow a check, and I don't like checks.

25...♖b8

26.♖a7 More direct was 26.♖xd6+ ♖xd6, and here, after 27.♗c5!, Black has no real defence: 27...♖e8 28.♖xe8

♗xe8 29.♗xd6 ♔xd6 30.♕xb7, and despite a lot of trades, White wins because he is now up two pawns.

26...♗e4 27.♕f7+ ♖e7 28.♕c4

28...♖c8? After hanging on for way too long, Shakh finally gives up. 28...♗xg2 29.♔xg2 ♕e5 would have kept the game going, but it would have been hopeless, of course. Fortunately, White can even win with very dumb play: 30.♔f1 ♕h2 31.♕b5+ ♔c8, and now 32.♖a4 is cool, but even 32.♕f5+ ♔d8 33.♕f3 keeps an extra pawn and a safer king.

29.♕a4+ ♗c6 30.♗xc6+ ♖xc6 31.♖c1

Black resigned. He is no longer able to defend his stuff, because there are too many pins.

∎ ∎ ∎

Inspirational draw

My favourite game of the event, incidentally, was a draw. Don't misunderstand me: I still think there is value in having winners in every bout, and as a spectator it's not fun when games end in 'peace'. But there are still draws, like the one between Carlsen and Aronian, that truly are inspirational. The quality of that game was incredible, with the players constantly playing better than the weak online engines following the game.

Magnus Carlsen
Levon Aronian
Zagreb 2019 (9)
Nimzo-Indian Defence, Ragozin Variation

1.d4 ♘f6 2.c4 e6 3.♘f3 d5 4.♘c3 ♗b4 5.♗g5 dxc4 6.e4 c5 7.e5 cxd4 8.♘xd4 ♗xc3+ 9.bxc3 ♕a5 10.exf6 ♕xg5 11.fxg7 ♕xg7 12.♕d2 0-0 13.♗xc4 ♖d8 14.♕e3 ♗d7

This position has been reached in over 50 serious chess games, and White almost always castles kingside. The game would continue along normal paths, but Black has managed to equalize pretty confidently. Carlsen has injected a new level of interest in many openings, and his next move is particularly aesthetically pleasing:

15.0-0-0!?
The king is clearly exposed on the queenside, but it is not easy to reach it. On the other hand, the plan of h4/♖h3 might be very annoying with an already open g-file. Also, in certain endgames, the king is simply better placed near the centre!

15...♘c6 16.♗b3 ♗e8!
More precise than the more natural alternative: 16...♖ac8 17.♔b2 would leave Black in a bit of trouble trying to find a useful move.

17.♘xc6 ♗xc6 18.h4 ♕f6! 19.♖h3

Levon Aronian's draw against Magnus Carlsen showed once again that also games 'without a result' can be fascinating epic struggles.

19...b5 A human move, trying to create counterplay on the queenside. Now ...b4 will always be annoying, although in the endgame, the weakness of c5 and the pawn on b5 might be costly.

20.♖g3+ ♔h8 21.♖g4!?

So ingenious! A double rook lift, if such a thing exists, to shoo the queen away from its powerful square on f6 and pressurize f7. Not to mention that it prevents ...b5-b4.

21...a5 22.♖f4 ♕g7 23.♖xd8+ ♖xd8 24.g4

Carlsen spots an idea: stick a rook on f6 and kill the queen on g7. Aronian foresees this idea, but realizes he has enough counterplay.

24...b4 25.g5 bxc3 25...♕xc3+? 26.♕xc3+ bxc3 27.♖xf7 is nearly hopeless. **26.♗c2** White is in no rush to capture the pawn. Once ♖f6 has been played, ♖h6 will be an issue now that the bishop has switched diagonals.

LENNART OOTES

26.♖f6 ♕f8 27.♕xc3 ♕a3+ is plenty of counterplay for Black, who has no need to trade queens in the ensuing complications.

26...♗d5 27.♖f6 ♕f8 28.♕xc3 ♖c8! The only move.

29.♕d3 Keeping the game going! 29.♖xf7+ ♖xc3 30.♖xf8+ ♔g7 31.♖f4 (otherwise ...♗e4) 31...e5 32.♖a4 ♗c6 33.♖g4 ♗d7 34.♖g3 ♖c4, and Black recovers his pawn on h4 (thanks to the threat of ...♗f5). The game should fizzle out to a draw.
29...♕g7 30.f4

White has clear and evil intentions: he is only a few moves away from constructing an ideal set-up by pushing the h-pawn, but he is one tempo short.
30...♔g8! 31.♔d2 After 31.h5, 31...h6! is the point. With the king on g8, ♖xh6 is not check, and White simply can't allow that queen on g7 to become active: his own king is too weak: 32.♖xh6 ♕a1+ 33.♔d2, and Black has options, but 33...♖xc2+ is a perpetual, to say the least.
After 31.♖h6?? f5! the h6-rook looks utterly silly.
31...h6

A cool opening, a titanic middlegame, and an endgame that fizzled out to a satisfying draw!

Without this idea, Black's position is simply paralyzed. Opening a file and an avenue for the queen is what will give Black the counterchances he needs.

32.a3! I would never have thought of this move. The control of b4 is important in some lines, and it forces Black to find a move.
32...hxg5 33.fxg5 ♖c4! Aronian is up to the job. Again, the pinning of the rook on f6 is important, and h4 is under attack. There are no issues on the back rank, because White has no good way to manoeuvre into it.
34.♕g3 Threatening the devastating ♕b8+, and Black again only has one resource, but it is enough.
34...♗e4 Forced again.

35.♗b3
35.♗xe4 ♖xe4 36.h5, and now:
– 36...♕f8 37.♕c7! could be surprisingly dangerous for Black, since the

queen can't leave the defence of f7 (thanks, a3!) and g6 is coming. The computer still manages to hold this, but only with very accurate play.
– 36...e5!, followed by ...♕f8, with a likely perpetual.
35...♖d4+ 36.♔e1 ♗f5 37.h5 ♖d3 38.♕b8+ ♕f8

In the end, simplifications are forced, and the resulting endgame is just a draw.
39.♕xf8+ ♔xf8 40.♗c2 ♖h3 41.♗xf5 exf5 42.h6 ♔g8 43.a4 ♖h4 44.♖xf5 ♖xa4 45.♔f2 ♖g4 46.♔f3 ♖g1 47.♔f2 ♖g4 48.♔f3 ♖g1 49.♔f2
What a spectacular struggle, with both sides finding great resources. It had a cool opening, a titanic middlegame struggle, and an endgame that fizzled out to a satisfying draw!

It seemed as if the tournament was going to climax in a fated duel in the penultimate round between So, as White and trailing by half a point, against Carlsen. One of the reasons that the splitting of the point can be so difficult for chess publicizing is that it sometimes produces absolute duds, and sometimes the most dramatic of games. In this case, I think, no blame can be placed on So for the approach he took against Carlsen. The clear goal of the GCT being to qualify for the final event in London in December, where everyone starts from scratch, it is important to accumulate as many GCT points as possible to clinch that spot. Only two classical events are part of this year's line-up, and they are considerably stronger in terms of GCT points than any of the Rapid and Blitz tournaments. Wesley So came, exchanged all the pieces, made a draw and secured a share of second place, even if everything went wrong against Aronian the next day. Besides, having the black pieces hasn't deterred Carlsen from beating up on people.

A point ahead of the field

Carlsen's last-round game made it seem like he has been playing the Grünfeld endgames all his life, whereas MVL, arguably the world's greatest expert of this defence, had just picked it up before the game to give it a try.

Magnus Carlsen's last-round win against arguably the world's greatest Grünfeld expert made it seem as if MVL had just picked up the opening to give it a try.

NOTES BY
Anish Giri

**Magnus Carlsen
Maxime Vachier-Lagrave**
Zagreb 2019 (11)
Grünfeld Indian, Exchange Variation

1.d4 ♘f6 2.c4 g6 3.♘c3 d5
It is a safe bet that MVL will go for his pet opening, the Grünfeld Defence.
4.♘f3 ♗g7 5.cxd5 ♘xd5 6.e4 ♘xc3 7.bxc3 c5 8.♗e3

One of the main systems against the Grünfeld. Carlsen had played it shortly before, so it didn't come as a complete surprise to Maxime, who deviated from his usual line of defence.
8...♕a5

The main line. Actually, Maxime has lately been going for the 8...♗g4 system, where it is certain that Magnus had something ready.
9.♕d2 ♘c6

10.♖b1 The point is to provoke ...a6 and only then go to c1 with the rook. Deep stuff.
10.♖c1 cxd4 11.cxd4 ♕xd2+ 12.♔xd2 0-0 13.d5 ♖d8 is supposed to be fine for Black if he knows a few more moves from here on in.
10...cxd4 A relatively fresh line, which caught my attention again when Jon-Ludvig Hammer, the other Norwegian, played it a few years back. Carlsen is obviously aware of this line, too.
After 10...a6 11.♖c1 cxd4 12.cxd4 ♕xd2+ 13.♔xd2 0-0 14.d5 ♖d8 the weakness of the b6-square matters: 15.♗b6.

11.cxd4 0-0 12.♕xa5 ♘xa5 13.♗d3 ♗g4 Black is hoping to create some quick play and challenge the d4-pawn. In such endgames it is often a matter of half a tempo and Black must be extremely precise if he wants to equalize.
14.0-0 Another critical move is 14.h3, but in view of Maxime's reply, this was certainly a good practical choice by Magnus.

14...♗xf3?
Maxime mis-remembered stuff. A tempo down, he comes too late to challenge White's pawn centre properly.
14...b6 is one of the moves suggested by the computer. It actually creates the amusing threat of 15...♗xf3 16.gxf3 and 16...♗xd4!, since the knight on a5 is not hanging after

17.♗xd4 ♖fd8 18.♗c3. This actually feels slow, but computers usually know what they are doing.

15.gxf3 e6 16.♖fd1
White obviously wants to keep his pawn mobility, but even 16.e5!?, followed by ♗e4, would have lead to a huge advantage.

16...♖fd8 17.♗f1

17...b6?! Black has no counter-play against the eventual d5 push. In addition, his a5-knight is really out of play here. However, 17...♖ac8 18.d5 exd5 19.exd5 b6 20.d6 was better.

17...♗f6! was the best move, intending to meet 18.d5 with 18...exd5 19.exd5 ♗e7!.

18.♗a6 18.♖bc1 was also very strong. **18...♖d6 19.♖bc1?!**
19.e5!? was very rough, cropping the a5-knight out of the game completely: 19...♖d7 20.♖dc1!.

19...♖ad8 20.♗g5!

A typical, yet always elegant, standard resource to blind the g7-bishop.

20...f6 21.♗e3 h6 21...♘c6! was called for, when at least the knight joins the defence.

22.♗b5 22.♖c7!? would have led to a winning endgame after 22...♘c6

23.d5 exd5 24.♖xd5 ♖xd5 25.exd5 ♘b4 26.♗c4 ♘xd5 27.♖xa7, and the b6-pawn falls, after which I assume White will just slowly queen the a-pawn.

22...f5? 22...g5! was a much better defensive attempt, with 23...f5! only after 23.h4. After 23.d5 exd5 24.♖c7 d4 Black is still fighting.

23.d5! After this push, ♗f4 is an important resource in all lines.

23...g5 A logical attempt to stop ♗f4, but now:

24.♗d2! fxe4 25.fxe4 a6 26.♗a4 exd5 27.♗b4!

The bishop disrupts the harmony between the black rooks along the d-file.

27...♖e6 28.♖xd5 ♖xd5 29.exd5
The d-pawn has a free pass now!

29...♖e4 30.♖c8+ ♔f7 31.a3

With the knight so out of touch, there is really no way to stop the runner on the d-file.

31...♗e5 32.♗e8+ ♔g7 33.d6 ♖d4 34.d7 ♘b7 35.♗e7 ♖e4 36.♗c6 ♗d4 37.♖c7

It wasn't too hard to remove the last defender of the magical d8-square, and now White's pawn will soon queen.
Black resigned.

■ ■ ■

Thus concluded another win for Carlsen, a point ahead of the field this time. His dominance was never in doubt, and even though he mentioned how tired he was at the closing ceremony, it was clear that his form had not suffered.

Maurice Ashley asked the winner's father, Henrik, what explained Magnus's return, stronger than ever, after what he described as a 'lull' from his peak of something like five years ago. Henrik Carlsen said something important: 'If we go back to the last period in which he [Magnus] was doing so well, it took us some time to appreciate how well everything had been working together'. He spoke of work, of willpower, of being a happy person, and of how many factors had to align to reach your theoretical max playing strength. Only someone very close to the World Champion can say what has sparked this resurgence, or whether he really is near his theoretical maximum. As a spectator and commentator, all I can say is that it is a pleasure to watch his chess. ■

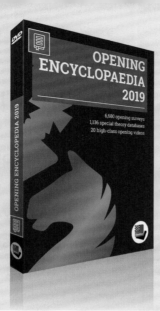

OPENING ENCYCLOPAEDIA 2019

NEW LAYOUT, BETTER ACCESS, EXCITING VIDEOS

The Encyclopaedia can help you learn openings rapidly giving you a head start against your next opponents. Each article includes explanations and annotated games, which illustrate typical plans, to help deepen your understanding.

The concept of the opening article: A Grandmaster or International Master presents you a repertoire idea, shows all important variations and his analyses, explains typical plans and shows all the critical lines. Every article includes annotated model games selected by the author to illustrate the ideas in tournament practice.

The new Opening Encyclopaedia 2019 was completely revamped to enhance usability, with features such as a new design, new menu, and opening name sorting for fast and easy access to your favorite openings. Under the Menu "Ideas for your Repertoire" you can find all articles classified according to the opening names: "Open games", "Semi-open games", "Closed games", "Half -closed game", "Flank-Openings" or "English Opening and Reti". E.g. for the popular Najdorf Variation the Opening Encyclopaedia offers 41 opening articles. Each of it is accessible easily via "Semi-open games"- Siclian Defence – Najdorf Variation. As easy the user can switch from one article to the other to absorb all the important maneuvers and typical plans related to the variation. That way finding your favorite openings becomes easy and fast! Additionally, the new Encyclopaedia offers the traditional access to find openings from the "ECO-list" as an alternative access to all opening articles.

Also new: 20 high-class opening videos are included in the Encyclopaedia 2019, from our popular ChessBase Authors. You'll find Daniel King, Simon Williams, Yannick Pelletier, Mihail Marin, Erwin l'Ami, presenting new opening ideas clear and vividly. The number of articles in the Opening Encyclopaedia is growing – it now contains more than 1,100 and the included games database contains all games from all the opening articles. This makes the new Opening Encyclopaedia 2019 an indispensable reference for every tournament player.

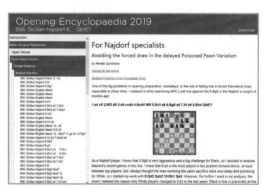

All innovations at a glance:

- Over 1,100 special theoretical databases
- 180 new opening surveys, a lot of them revised, in total 6,680 surveys
- Over 38,000 illustrative games
- Much improved usability: New design, new menu, new sorting of openings according to names for a fast and comfortable access
- 20 opening videos (total duration: 7 hours) of the most popular ChessBase Authors

Opening Encyclopaedia 2019 **99,90 €**

Update from
Opening Encyclopaedia 2018 **59,90 €**

ChessBase GmbH · News: en.chessbase.com · CB Shop: shop.chessbase.com
CHESSBASE DEALER: NEW IN CHESS · P.O. Box 1093 · NL-1810 KB Alkmaar
phone (+31)72 5127137 · fax (+31)72 5158234 · WWW.NEWINCHESS.COM

And then Magnus created
a chess club

JONATHAN TISDALL explains why the World Champion's actions away from the chessboard suddenly made headlines and caused controversy in his home country.

How a bitter feud about gambling may revolutionize chess in Norway

Magnus Carlsen's seemingly endless streak of victories makes for pleasant reading in chess-mad Norway, but no one was prepared when he suddenly made the news outside the tournament arena. Many were puzzled when the World Champion killed a bid to stage a title defence in his home country, and even more so when he got involved in a national muck-flinging contest over the gambling industry.

Magnus then risked widespread dishonour and disrepute... by starting a chess club. For non-Norwegians many ingredients in the conflict may be unfamiliar, so let me try to shed a bit of light on these recent developments.

Carlsen's refusal to support a bid to stage the world title match in Stavanger was easy to understand. He said that he felt playing in Norway, but far from his literal home turf in the Oslo area, would mean undesirable additional pressure on him. In the background, but included in his public explanation, was Magnus'

displeasure with the way the federation had ignored his wishes during the bid-mounting process, and this was perhaps the more compelling explanation.

The other 'scandal', which I have dubbed Kindred-gate, was the proposal that Norway's chess federa-

tion (NSF) lobby for an end to the state monopoly on gambling, and for a licensing system of the kind that neighbours Sweden and Denmark have adopted. Kindred is a conglomerate of 11 of Europe's leading online gambling companies, with Unibet probably the best-known of the bunch, and Kindred would pay the NSF roughly NOK 50 million (currently just over five million euro) over five years for their lobbying.

Thanks to my nomadic background of USA to Norway via the UK, I got regular requests for explanation during this furore from baffled onlookers who live in places where gambling and betting are just mundane, everyday activities, and where state monopolies and benefits might be puzzling concepts. A crash course in some relevant aspects of Norwegian chess – and life – is necessary, and a quick explanation of my particular viewpoint is probably helpful as well.

When I heard this proposal, I expected (rightly) that the result would be the closest thing possible to chess civil war. It was guaranteed to violently polarize opinion, and particularly alienate traditional, established opinion. It turned old friends, all of whom wanted nothing but the best for the game here, against each other. It involved a range of volatile, emotional topics, political, ethical and more. To further fuel the fire, there was an ongoing national debate about the causes and alarming levels of gambling addiction here, with a focus on legal attempts to fight foreign companies advertising and operating in Norway.

The debate offered a wide range of hills for people to die on, and limited hope of calm discussion, especially in our modern 'social' media climate. I looked at this as someone who had seen aspects of the debate from a multitude of angles; who grew up in the individualistic US of A, but had now spent most of my life in radically different Norway; worked as a mainstream journalist, in corporate communications, and inside the impoverished chess federation; and had seen how fundamentally important the many local volunteer chess enthusiasts are here.

I could easily understand why such an incendiary idea – roughly NOK

When I heard this proposal, I expected (rightly) that the result would be the closest thing possible to chess civil war.

10 million a year for a rather vague commitment to help legalize an open gambling market in Norway – would be, and probably would have to be, handled quietly and secretly until it was ready to ignite. I am aware that even the pro-Kindred faction could admit seeing problems with the way that the proposal was rolled out and timed – just a month before a Congress vote at the annual general assembly of the chess federation. In the wake of the mismanagement of the title match bid negotiations, which caused a seething internal rift in the federation board, it didn't help to prevent a controversial cause seeing the light of day in a manner that could easily appear conspiratorial.

The Carlsen Effect
I like to explain the bizarre status of chess here in Norway by relating the astonishment of a visitor who is first stunned to see live prime-time, move-by-move chess coverage on national television, only to go into total shock when noticing that the tiny news ticker at the bottom of the screen is showing English Premier League football results. Live coverage of the Carlsen-Nakamura Fischer Random match was televised against the *Winter* Olympics – in *Norway*!

Chess sets literally sold out across the country during Magnus' title match in 2013, beginners books began to be stocked in supermarkets, national productivity dips when he plays, Oslo's dedicated chess pub

The Good Knight has become a hip drinking spot for all. But – didn't I say the federation was impoverished? Membership, funding and sponsorship has not had the expected benefits, although chess in schools and certain projects have. But card-carrying federation growth, not so much.

Club chess continues to depend on a particularly Norwegian concept – *dugnad*. This is a kind of semi-compulsory community spirit that can cover anything from being roped into doing fund-raising duties despite paying dues for your kid's sports activity, to the kind of past miracle in which a group builds a newlywed couple's house during their wedding party.

Principles over cash
In very recent memory, the Norwegian federation voted against becoming part of the sports system, which would have entitled it to regular, and relatively generous, state funding. The reason, believe it or not: Norway frowns on competitive pressure on children, and chess becoming a sport would effectively mean that kids would have to be delayed in their chess development, an impossible situation in an increasingly 'younger' game.

The lure of financial stability was very tempting for a federation operating on a shoestring – and would there ever be another Magnus-scale talent that would suffer from this compromise? One important footnote (not that it was an issue at the time): Norwegian sport is the major recipient of funding from Norsk Tipping (NT)... the state gambling monopoly.

Norway has a state monopoly on vices like alcohol and gambling. The country is also noted for its lifelong health service, its fully free education system, its very generous maternity and paternity leave, and so on. This something-for-money arrangement means that Norwegians are traditionally relatively happy taxpayers.

Lotteries have been defined as a tax for the stupid, and here it is very easy to feel tempted to be stupid – state gambling funds culture and humanitarian causes as well as sport, including aid for gambling addicts. You can also earmark a bit of your wager for a chosen cause – so every time I decide to be taxed for daydreaming of swimming in gold coins, I can make sure a bit of it goes to my chess club. And here is another tricky element in the equation: Norsk Tipping's vast investment and exposure in the national media – constant advertising and cooperative projects bolster the newspapers, and the state broadcaster NRK televises the major lottery draws. All these factors give NT an entrenched position and a subtly positive aura. When the Kindred debate inevitably went public, the weight of the coverage was predictably

a sponsor of the last title match in London. But the Kindred deal was 'even worse' – it was money for *lobbying*. How on earth could that not be seen as political activity?

This seemed to me to be the most obvious hill to die on – gambling was not just a highly divisive issue; contemplating lobbying for it appeared to violate the essence of the federation's foundation. Moral arguments that purported to see gambling money as evil (or wonderful depending on who donated it…) could nevertheless be a hill for others.

The state of modern debate is ugly at the best of times, and in an argument in which most minds were firmly made up in advance, tempers were regularly frayed. Apparently frustrated with the level of abuse and the

State gambling funds culture and humanitarian causes as well as sport, including aid for gambling addicts.

hostile, and when Magnus decided to support the Kindred deal he was by no means immune to tacit accusations of links to the gambling industry.

Norwegian sporting heroes tend to be quite bullet-proof when it comes to their popularity, but bucking the establishment seemed to be possibly more controversial, image-wise, than, say, drunk-driving by winter sports athletes.

Even worse
To be honest, I thought the debate at the federation level was likely to fall at the first hurdle; the NSF is defined as a non-political organization, and this is an essential part of its charter and inclusivity. Kindred sponsorship would have been controversial enough: but one of its arms, Unibet, has been an unnamed sponsor of Norway Chess in the past, and was

lack of meaningful dialogue with just under two weeks to go before the Congress vote, Magnus took action.

The World Champion founded a new chess club, Offerspill (a typical Magnus play on words: *offer* can mean sacrifice or victim, and *spill*: play or gamble) and promised to pay the federation registration fees for the first 1000 members. Since it was clearly stating that members should understand that they were joining a club that would back the Kindred deal, this was interpreted as an attempt to hijack the Congress vote by buying a voting bloc. The result was a wave of unprecedented media vitriol for Magnus.

A question of motive
The champ was accused of trying to exploit an administrative loophole to generate delegates, which he denied,

I believe the formation of OSK will go down as a brilliant manoeuvre, reminiscent of Carlsen's often baffling, infuriating and effective bits of late title match strategy.

claiming he was fighting to create better conditions for emerging and future players, either by Kindred or by club. I believe the formation of OSK (Offerspill SjakKlubb) will go down as a brilliant manoeuvre, reminiscent of Carlsen's often baffling, infuriating and effective bits of late title match strategy. It might appear dubious, but will be judged on results.

The club was swamped with online registrants and exceeded the 1000-member mark in hours. With OSK having the potential to sway the coming vote, the 'no' side was galvanized into action and reaction, and their unified turnout would eventually mean that the Kindred deal was doomed, all the more so when OSK voluntarily chose to limit their delegates to pre-existing and transferred federation members, and those paying dues.

The fallout generated headlines for days, as this was now followed by the typical legal circus (the nation's leading expert on this type of dispute opined that the new club's members should not have voting rights at the upcoming Congress, while other experts laid down conflicting rulings, based on the first expert's teachings, etc.).

A different angle actually produced shock waves within 'chess Norway' – the revelation that a remarkable number of Norway's emerging talent had defected from their clubs to join OSK in solidarity with the beating Magnus was taking over trying to secure funding for the game. Suddenly, local clubs were listening – how fed up were the kids, and how much of this squabble might be a generational conflict over dated priorities?

The Effect *is* Magnus

The controversial timing of project OSK meant that almost no one noticed the seismic effects of Magnus forming his own club, sceptics being too busy with loud cries of conspiracy, and convinced in advance that freeloader members would never renew. Quality checking the registry list kept the club in the news after the Norwegian Prime Minister's name turned up as a bogus member. In the end, the number of real members was still over the 1000 'invitees' on the books.

Magnus had attracted interest from young talents, 'other gamers' (especially poker players, I believe), and most importantly, that mystical demographic – people who know the rules, sometimes barely, and just want to play, now more than in just an app or online.

In hours, he had created a club that formed a sizeable percentage of the federation – which, in 2019, had dipped to around just 3400 members. He had solved the federation conundrum of how to grow under Magnus – *be Magnus*.

OSK is a unique creature – a club with international membership that aims to have a 'bricks and mortar' presence. Facing the logistical problems of success, they have been active via lichess.org, but intend to field teams in the Norwegian leagues. Magnus plays online every week, and one of their board members told me that they plan to expand to other platforms, establish training sessions between selected top players, stream, produce learning material and set up physical clubs. Thanks to Magnus, there are natural partners like Chess24 and Play Magnus, and

I don't see why there aren't all sorts of possible new synergies – perhaps even with existing clubs, which might be able to help create a physical presence throughout the far-flung country.

I've been asked for OSK info for Indian prodigy Nihal Sarin and his trainer Srinath Narayanan, who were also captivated by the idea of having Magnus as a regular club mate and possible sparring partner, something that OSK found equally exciting...

And if Magnus spends a bit of time on regular promotions for the club, how easily can OSK expand in size? There can be no complaints about its legitimacy if it succeeds in its ambitions, and it could conceivably become a federation within the federation, not least in terms of voting power.

The future?

To me, OSK was an instant symbol of Magnus' creativity and fervour for the game and the kids he's inspiring, as well as of a new, evolving platform that I am not sure the traditional forces here will be able to keep up with. But for those with the energy to fight these messy battles, on either side, there will be opportunity afterwards.

When the public spectacle finally resulted in a victory against Kindred, the chess community ended up pleasing the establishment, and a dialogue with politicians about the possibility of the NSF reaching a special type of sporting agreement with dispensation for young players is suddenly a talking point.

If successful, perhaps organized chess in Norway will get another shot at the kind of funding it so desperately needs. Of course, this could mean a new round of bitter argument about the ethics of gambling money, now that we can no longer ignore where the sports' funding comes from. Will Norwegian chess once again talk itself out of a financial deal? What are the odds? ∎

MAXIMize your Tactics

with Maxim Notkin

Find the best move in the positions below

Solutions on page 65

1. Black to play

2. White to play

3. White to play

4. White to play and hold the draw

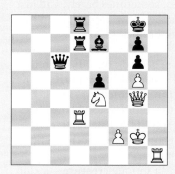

5. White to play

6. White to play

7. White to play

8. White to play

9. White to play

The meteoric rise of Gukesh

Will the super-talent be the next Indian World Champion?

India is enjoying a chess boom of rare dimensions, and Chennai is the country's undeniable chess capital. Perhaps the greatest talent from the southern Indian metropolis to follow in the footsteps of the great Vishy Anand is 13-year-old Dommaraju Gukesh, the second youngest grandmaster in history.
V. SARAVANAN met the prodigy at his home and spoke to his parents and coach.

FREDERIC FRIEDEL

The brand-new GM is feted by S. Kailasanathan (the CEO of his sponsor Microsense), Indian legend Manuel Aaron, and D.V. Sundar of the All India Chess Federation.

For Indian parents and coaches, the 'target' for their children's chess these days is breaking Sergey Karjakin's record of attaining the grandmaster title in 12 years and seven months. That record still stands, but Dommaraju Gukesh came close, though he ultimately had to settle for becoming the second youngest ever at 12 years, seven months and 17 days, bettering the record of his countryman Pragg-nanandhaa by about three months.

Gukesh's rise to the title was truly meteoric. Starting in September 2017, when he scored his first IM norm in Malaysia, he amassed 185 rating points, scored three IM and GM norms and played a total of 276 rated games in 30 tournaments in a row. The successful completion of his grandmaster title came at the Delhi Open in January of this year.

Having achieved this landmark, he didn't exactly rest on his laurels. He didn't slow down at all, playing one event after the other in India and crisscrossing Europe. In the seven months after obtaining the GM title, he played 116 games, reaching a peak rating of 2543 in June.

'Very normal'

What makes Gukesh tick? What makes him play such an inhuman amount of chess and keeps him climbing the charts? To find out, I visited him and his parents at their home in Chennai and spoke to his coach, Vishnu Prasanna, a GM who is known for his diligence and profound ideas about the game. He sums up Gukesh's qualities as 'remarkable positional understanding, being very driven and focussed on his goals, fearlessness, thirst for knowledge, and the ability to understand chess concepts and apply them in his own games'.

Vishnu remembers how, in an early training session, he showed his pupil a position from an old Smyslov game, in which the former World Champion had conducted a deep and rather unexpected rook manoeuvre. Much to his surprise, Gukesh found the move instantly, terming it 'very normal'.

Ever since they started working in the middle of 2017, this ability to understand positional nuances was the most remarkable aspect of Gukesh's chess, says Vishnu. Especially his maturity in understanding positional concepts, his pure 'chess sense', startled Vishnu many times. 'Whenever I showed him an interesting position, he always came up with remarkable ideas, while it took longer or simply proved impossible for other kids to find them. His natural instincts are super-positional.'

Gukesh also has another remarkable side to his chess: the ability of 'being' rather than 'doing' on the board. Jonathan Rowson's excellent *Chess for Zebras* advocates the chess equivalent of 'mindfulness' on the board, in which the maxim 'Don't do something, just sit in there!' takes preference. Over the chessboard, this takes the form of 'being adaptive,

> **In the seven months after obtaining the Grandmaster title, Gukesh played 116 games, reaching a peak rating of 2543.**

letting things happen, absorbing pressure, taking it easy', as defined by Rowson.

Vishnu and Gukesh worked on it extensively, with the games of Topalov and Carlsen as their material. Vishnu claims the concept

GM Vishnu Prasanna started working with Gukesh in the middle of 2017. 'The kid is running at a very fast pace!'

of 'being' is at a well-refined stage in Gukesh's play, especially as he doesn't like weakening his position. And curiously enough, they selected two players from different ends of the spectre: Carlsen, tightening screws on his opponent with deep positional principles, and Topalov, sacrificing material and then waiting for his opponent to crack up in the resulting tactical melee.

A striking example of 'being' is the game that Gukesh played against French GM Matthieu Cornette in the French league this year, which Gukesh himself claims to be one of his best games so far. You will find it at the end of this article, with his own notes.

Concepts

Gukesh and his trainer also work on 'concepts': any element of playing chess that can be understood with deep study and applied to your games, e.g. different kinds of flows of thinking over the chessboard: when should you calculate or when just make moves going with the strategic flow? When should you look for long lines in a position, and when should you keep it simple?

For this they choose a particular player and observe how he conducts a particular aspect of his chess. For instance, they studied Maxim Vachier-Lagrave's openings, noting that, for a top-class player, Vachier-Lagrave has a surprisingly modest repertoire. They observed during their study that due to the narrowness of his repertoire, he occasionally gets into difficult positions, but almost always comes out unscathed. How he extricates himself out of such difficult corners, is a concept.

Another concept is to study players with different over-the-board styles and psychologies. How the modern players approach the game. 'I really like the way Ding Liren plays his chess – dynamic but not rash, and very sound play all around,' says Gukesh.

Model parents

Vishnu also credits Gukesh's rise to his parents and the amount of effort and sacrifice shown by the family, calling them 'model parents'. When I sit down and chat with Rajnikanth and Padmakumari at their home at Korattur, a quiet area in the outskirts of Chennai, it is obvious that here is a family who have rearranged their lives drastically and willingly in the last few years to ensure that their son can pursue his passion.

Dr. Dommaraju Rajinikanth is an ear, nose & throat surgeon who has almost sacrificed his career to travel with Gukesh ever since things got serious. Dr. Padma Kumari is an Assistant Professor who works at the State Government Medical College at Chennai as a microbiologist, also teaching her subject to resident student doctors at the attached medical college.

The ride over the past few years has not been very smooth for the couple, because no one in their family was employed outside academia and absolutely no one in sports. So, ever since Gukesh learnt the game in school as an extracurricular activity at six years of age, and showed promise by the age of seven, the parents have gone beyond their means to look after his passion and early talent.

The Velammal group of schools have been a big boon for the chess players of Chennai. They allow their students to pursue chess and do not bother them with demands of attendance to classes, allowing them to attend examinations directly. Besides Gukesh, the illustrious alumni – and current students – of Velammal include a long list of chess players, with Adhiban, Sethuraman, Murali Karthikeyan, Aravindh Chithambaram and Praggnanandhaa the most prominent.

A life of only chess

But taking the decision to skip school and concentrate on playing chess tournaments, which meant almost

Gukesh's father, a surgeon, and his mother, a microbiologist, have rearranged their lives drastically in the last few years to ensure that their son can pursue his passion.

foregoing their monthly income in order to attend to their son, was a huge decision for his parents to make. Both Rajinikanth and Padma-

With journalists, he used to answer in monosyllables, or in sign language!

kumari swear that it was very tough, a decision taken purely because of the passion and promise shown by Gukesh from the very beginning. They initially decided to take the plunge for a period of one full year, 'not planning much about the future and letting fate take its course', as they say.

Two of the trickiest issues were the worry that their only son might miss

out on a normal childhood because of not attending school, and the financial need of providing for playing tournaments in Europe, which went beyond their reduced monthly income and ate into their life savings.

Rajinikanth also mentions Gukesh's inability to express himself to outsiders clearly till about 2017. 'With journalists, he used to answer in monosyllables, or in sign language! Most of the time, I had to sit with him to answer on his behalf. These were things a school education would have given him. Being limited to a life of only chess and tournaments from the age of around eight, he was always very shy.'

This was also a period when Gukesh struggled with time-pressure over the board, spoiling tournaments because of a single loss in the initial rounds and such. But having down-to-earth parents from a hardworking background slowly helped mould his chess career.

The Short incident

One of the incidents highlighting Rajinikanth's balanced temperament was when Gukesh defeated Nigel Short in the Bangkok Open in 2018. Short was two pawns up in an ending with rooks and opposite-coloured bishops in a seemingly winning position.

Gukesh-Short
Bangkok 2018
position after 58...♖a2+

Here, having played 58...♖a2+, Short forgot to press the clock, which Gukesh noticed. Just as any other 11-year-old *might* do, he didn't alert his opponent but waited for his clock to run out of time, thus winning the game. To make it even worse, he got excited when the flag fell, stood up and called the arbiter to claim his point. An annoyed Short left the table without signing the score sheet, while Gukesh even ran after him to get his signed.

A furious Short wrote on his Facebook page: 'Lose with dignity they say. I will try better next time –

An annoyed Short left the table without signing the score sheet, while Gukesh even ran after him to get his signed.

although it is a bit hard when your opponent is fully aware that you have not pressed your cock (in a winning position) and jumps up and down with glee the moment your flag falls.'

Rajinikanth's response to Short's post was suitably mature and expressed regret about the incident: 'Extremely sorry and equally disappointed that a well-fought game ended in such an embarrassing manner in the end... But kindly excuse (Gukesh's) immediate getting up after the flag (fell) ... as he was totally overawed playing you and getting a lucky win... Apologies on his behalf. But (I) request everyone to kindly spare a thought for him ... It is quite natural to be overawed by the occasion of playing a legend and fighting almost close to 6 hrs and standing his ground, and then unexpectedly something bizarre like this happen(s)'.

Sponsorship

When I ask his parents how things are currently on the financial front, they are more than relieved that it has all worked out fine by now. Apart from sponsorship by the Velammal school, Gukesh has been assured of sponsorship by *Microsense Private Limited*, a Chennai-based company whose Managing Director Kailasanathan is an ardent chess lover. Rajinikanth happily admits that there has also been hint of further sponsorships, now that Gukesh's achievement has attracted wide publicity in the country, and the future looks much better than the past.

A typical kid

How is Gukesh at home? The parents chuckle that he is a typical kid, emotional and very attached to the family, with a different demeanour at home compared to his public posturings. He insists on his mother to hand-feed him, prefers to be told mythological stories at bedtime rather than reading on his own, and jumps around on drawing

Dommaraju Gukesh

Born: May 29, 2006,
Chennai, India

Career highlights

2013:	Learns to play chess
2015:	Gold at U-9 World Schools
2017:	Malaysia, first IM Norm
2018:	Moscow Open, second IM norm
	Cappelle-la-Grande, final IM norm
	5 gold medals at the Asian Youth Championships
	Under-12 World Champion
	Bangkok Open, first GM norm
	Paracin, Serbia, second GM norm
2019:	Delhi, final GM norm
	Second youngest GM ever at 12 years, 7 months, 27 days
	Reaches his highest rating of 2543 in June

At home Gukesh is a typical kid, who loves to jump around on furniture and play cricket and badminton.

room furniture. He plays cricket and badminton inside the house with other members of his extended family and accompanies his grandfather on evening walks.

But the shy character has changed a lot in the past year or so. His confidence has grown ever since he tasted success over the chessboard and he consistently practices Meditation. Gukesh is much more at ease dealing with the press now, and is quite controlled with his emotions. Gukesh admits: 'I was really determined to beat Karjakin's record by making a GM norm at the Sitges Open in December 2018, and was quite disappointed that I couldn't achieve my aim. But I recovered from the emotion in a couple of hours'.

'Nowadays, when he loses a game, he plays the next game vigorously, unlike earlier. He has much more aggression and is pretty confident about his chess now,' says Rajini-

kanth. The best example is the way he conducted the game which yielded him the grandmaster title.

Dommaraju Gukesh
Dinesh Kumar Sharma
New Delhi 2019

position after 11...♘f7

It was a different Gukesh who walked to the board for this game, because he played aggressively from the word go and, in the middlegame, went in for the kill in great style.

12.♘f4?! 12.♗e3 or 12.b3 would have given White a typical edge on the white side of a French Defence.
12...♘xd4 13.♘h5 ♘xf3+?
14.♕xf3 White has ample compensation for the pawn, and Gukesh conducts the game in a style we rarely see from him.
14...♗e5 15.♗e3 ♕d8? 16.♗c5 The black king is in real danger and White only needs to find precise tactics to win.
16...♗d7 17.♖fe1 ♕c7? 18.♖ac1 ♖c8 19.♕g4 g6

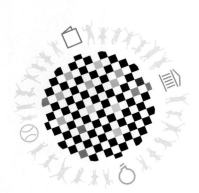

White is winning, but the finish is still something to appreciate.

20.♘g7+! ♗xg7 21.♖xe6+!

21...♔d8 After 21...♗xe6 22.♕xe6+ ♔d8 23.♗e7+ it will be mate soon: 23...♔e8 (or very soon: 23...♕xe7 24.♖xc8 mate) 24.♗b5+ ♕c6 25.♗c5+ ♔d8 26.♕e7 mate.

22.♗e7+ ♔e8 23.♗d6+ ♔d8 24.♗xc7+ ♖xc7 25.♖xc7 ♔xc7 26.♕f4+ Black resigned.

Headspinning complications

I ask Gukesh if he enjoyed playing this way. With a shy smile and the typically evolving voice of a 13-year-old, Gukesh admits that he did. But when I ask him about the reason for this transformation, he typically replies 'I don't know!', hinting of the kid inside him.

Then he says about the increased aggression in his game, 'Last June, I decided to play the Sveshnikov. We were packing to go to Russia, and I was getting bored. I still don't know why I decided to play it. Probably from studying the games from the Carlsen-Caruana match. I called my coach and told him, I have decided to play the Sveshnikov. He laughed and said, fine, carry on!'

He used to play the Réti with White and the Caro-Kann and Slav with the black pieces, but now he is expanding his repertoire, going for the Sveshnikov and the King's Indian. Why? 'Because I really like playing "crazy" positions, with headspinning complications. But I know that I can play them only if I prepare my openings thoroughly. I really look forward to doing that in future,' he says confidently.

As I reflect on this statement, I see Vishnu's point behind his assessment of Gukesh that he is a responsible kid. Who understands that if he has to get something, he has to work towards that.

The future

So what does the future hold? Gukesh is typically full of his plans. He wants to prepare his openings, work on his calculation, which he feels is still open to much improvement, and to play lots of strong events.

For Vishnu Prasanna things are also clear: 'The kid is running at a very fast pace! I need not sit with him every day now to develop anything for him. I think he can go all the way, to the very top. But I don't want him to chase things. You have to be interested in chess. There should be a passion for the game, a desire to understand its mystery. And you succeed once you do.'

Without a doubt, Gukesh seems firmly set on that course.

NOTES BY
Dommaraju Gukesh

Dommaraju Gukesh
Matthieu Cornette
Brest 2019
Réti Opening, Reversed Benoni

I was invited to be a part of the Cannes Chess Club at this year's French League. This was my first experience in being invited for a league and I was excited to play and do well, as it gave me the opportunity to face off against strong European Grandmasters.

1.♘f3 d5 2.g3

The Réti/King's Indian Attack has been a constant in my repertoire for the last couple of years.

2...♘f6 3.♗g2 c5 4.0-0 e6

Before the game I was a bit confused about whether to go for my favourite KIA with 5.d3 or for the line I played in the game.

5.c4 d4 6.e3 ♘c6 7.exd4 cxd4

7...♘xd4?! is not a good exchange for Black: 8.♘xd4 ♕xd4 (8...cxd4 9.d3 ♗d6 10.b4! is also better for White) 9.d3 ♗e7 10.♘c3 0-0 11.♗e3 ♕d6 12.♕e2 e5 13.h3 ♗e6 14.♖fe1, with a white edge in Aronian-Shirov, Switzerland 2016 (1-0, 32).

8.d3

8...♗d6 It was easy to predict that my opponent would go for this system with Black. He had already played this system in the past.
The critical move is 8...♗e7 9.♘a3!? 0-0 10.♖e1 ♖e8 11.♗f4 ♗b4 12.♖e2, when the rook looks a little awkward, but preventing Black from playing ...e5 is more important: 12...♘h5 13.♗g5 ♗e7 14.♗xe7 ♕xe7 15.♕d2 ♖d8 16.♘c2 a5 17.♘e5, and White was better in Wang Hao-Xu Yinglun, China 2013 (1-0, 46).

9.♗g5 h6 10.♗xf6 ♕xf6 11.♘bd2

11...♕e7 Less strong is 11...0-0?! 12.♘e4 ♕e7 13.♘xd6 ♕xd6 14.♖e1! e5 15.b4, and White has a pleasant plus.

12.a3 a5 13.♘e4 ♗c7
All this has been seen before.

14.c5
Interesting is 14.b4!? axb4 (after 14...f5?, 15.♘h4! is problematic) 15.axb4 ♖xa1 16.♕xa1 ♕xb4 17.♖b1 ♕e7 18.♘xd4 ♘xd4 19.♕xd4 0-0 20.♕c5!?, but the position should be tenable for Black after 20...♕d7.
14...0-0 15.♘fd2 f5 15...♗d7?! 16.♘c4, with the e4-knight coming to d6, is really unpleasant for Black.
16.♘d6 ♗xd6 17.cxd6 ♕xd6

Both me and my opponent were prepared up to this point, but we had come to different conclusions about the assessment of the position. My opponent had prepared the same position with the white pieces, but he considered it equal and harmless for Black.
18.♘c4 ♕c7 19.♖e1
This position I had still looked at in my preparation. White has given a pawn for the e5-square and it is not clear what Black is going to do with the c8-bishop. Although objectively

Black should be fine, I thought practically it is a little unpleasant for him.
19...♗d7 20.♖c1 ♖a6 21.♖e2!
With the idea of playing ♕e1-b4, with ♖ec2 also possible in some lines.
This was the first idea I spotted after my opponent went 20...♖a6. The longer I looked at it, the more attractive it looked for White and I decided to go for it.

21...♖e8?! Better seemed 21...f4!?, with the idea of stopping White from playing f4: 22.♗e4 ♗e8! 23.♖ec2 ♘e7!?.

22.♕e1!

The continuation to 21.♖e2. White's pieces are optimally placed to aim at e6 and also for White to play b4 at an opportune moment.

22...♕b8 23.f4

I was in no hurry to force anything and understood that I could patiently improve my position. Black has to play pretty creatively to untangle his position and activate his pieces.

23...b5? Better was 23...a4!, stopping White from playing b4, when 24.♘d2?! can be met by 24...e5!.

24.♘d2 a4 Here 24...e5? is not good in view of 25.♘b3.

25.b4!

This is the problem with 23...b5.

25...♕d6? 25...axb3 26.♘xb3 looks pretty bad for Black, with ♘c5 coming next: 26...♖xa3 27.♘c5.

It was still not too late for 25...e5! 26.♖c5! exf4 27.♖xe8+ ♕xe8 28.♕xe8+ ♗xe8 29.♖xb5 fxg3 30.hxg3, and although the position is better for White now, Black should have played this. Black's position lacks the harmony to defend against White's racing b-pawn.

26.♘f3!

After this move it is total domination.

26...♖c8 27.♖ec2 ♖a7 28.♘e5 ♖ac7 29.♘xc6! ♗xc6

30.♕e5!

This is the move my opponent had missed when he went 27...♖a7. Black

At the start of his game against Kherlen Tamir from Mongolia at the 2018 Asian Youth Championships, where Gukesh won 5 gold medals.

is in a state of permanent paralysis now.

30...♕d7 31.h4! With the idea of ♔h2 and ♖xc6, when Black cannot take on c1 with check.

31.♖xc6?? would be premature because of 31...♖xc6 32.♕xb5 ♖xc1+.

31...♔f7?? Losing immediately, but Black's position was beyond saving anyway. After 31...♔f8 32.♕c5+ ♔e8 33.♕b6 Black loses a piece.

32.♗xc6 ♖xc6 33.♕xb5

Black resigned.

I was very happy with my win and with the way the game progressed, and especially with my main idea, ♖e2 and ♕e1. ■

Both me and my opponent were prepared up to this point, but we had come to different conclusions.

Armageddon in a Riga Library

Mamedyarov claims second FIDE GP

Once again Shakhriyar Mamedyarov proved what an unpredictable force he is. After he had been eliminated in the first round of the Moscow Grand Prix, the Azeri star bounced back with a win in the Riga GP, defeating Maxime Vachier-Lagrave in a long and tense final. **VLADIMIR BARSKY** reports from the birthplace of the great Mikhail Tal.

NIKI RIGA

The second leg of the FIDE Grand Prix was hosted by the capital of Latvia, which for many generations of chess players is associated above all with the 'Magician from Riga' Mikhail Tal. Scenes from a 1960 newsreel immediately come to mind: the crowded railway station, where the 8th World Champion, only 23 years old, arrives after his victory over Botvinnik. He is greeted by a storm of applause, he is carried aloft and he floats above the crowd...

Of course, the organizers wanted to pay tribute to the memory of Mikhail Tal, and so in parallel with the Grand Prix stage there were impressive rapid and blitz tournaments, and also a 'Riga holidays' junior tournament. The juniors even competed in the same building, the Latvian National Library, and they were able to watch the play of the modern heroes of the chess world and collect autographs and selfies.

The library itself, which was built on the banks of the Daugava opposite the historic city centre, creates a strong impression with its size and ultra-modern architecture. For chess it was simply ideally appro-

priate and for tournaments under the World Chess aegis this was practically a breakthrough: the grandmasters played not in an 'aquarium' behind sound-proof glass, but on a normal stage in a spacious auditorium. Perhaps there is no such thing as new?

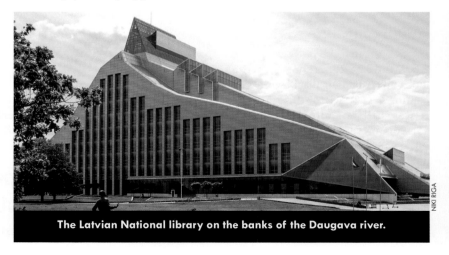

The Latvian National library on the banks of the Daugava river.

NIKI RIGA

An impression of the stage during the first round when all 16 participants were still present.

There was also a VIP lounge, but it was practically empty: with rare exceptions, the only persons there were the members of the Appeals Committee and the players' seconds. In Moscow, in the Central Chess Club, there were far more people, but there one of the sponsors was 'Beluga' vodka, and you could try various cocktails. A coincidence? Possibly... Only on the day of the final tie-break did it become lively in the Riga VIP lounge, when Dana Reiznitse-Ozola, a strong chess player and a minister in the Latvian government, arrived there with her husband and three young children (while her older daughter worked at the tournament as a volunteer).

I should remind you that the FIDE Grand Prix consists of four knock-out tournaments: the first took place in May in Moscow (where in the final Ian Nepomniachtchi defeated Alexander Grischuk), and the third and fourth stages will be held in November in Hamburg and in December in Tel Aviv. Twenty-two grandmasters are participating in the series, and each has three attempts.

I should also remind you that, according to the new rules, the pairings are made just a couple of hours before the start of the tour-nament and without any particular deference to ratings (there are only four 'seeds'). Thanks to this, on the one hand, no one can prepare in advance for an opponent, and, on the other hand, in the very first round pairings are sometimes made

between players who, in a different scenario, could well have met in the final. The battle is extremely fierce, and already in the first round two matches went to the Armageddon.

The first round

On the day of the first games a head-line-making event for the chess world occurred: at a tournament in France

The grandmasters played not in an 'aquarium' behind sound-proof glass, but on a normal stage in a spacious auditorium.

grandmaster Igor Rausis was 'caught red-handed'. In the last few years he has been representing the Czech Republic, and the strongest grand-master of this country, David Navara, who reacts sensitively to any injus-tice, obviously took this entire ugly cheating episode very much to heart. I was told that at breakfast Navara did not want to talk about anything other than this episode, returning to it all the time. To be honest, this was not the best frame of mind before a difficult encounter of your own – and he faced playing Black against the rating favourite of the tournament.

Maxime Vachier-Lagrave
David Navara
Riga 2019 (1.1)
Caro-Kann, Two Knights Variation

1.e4 c6 2.♘f3 d5 3.♘c3 ♗g4 4.h3 ♗xf3 5.♕xf3 ♘f6 6.♗e2 e6 7.0-0 ♗c5 8.♖d1 ♗d4 9.♕f4!?

We will not delve into the opening subtleties, but merely mention that the Two Knights Variation against the Caro-Kann Defence is firmly in the repertoire of Etienne Bacrot, who was helping MVL in Riga. Now the battle revolves around the d2-d4 advance.

The gambit continuation in the game is not a novelty; it was introduced last year. Nevertheless, to all appearances, for Navara it came as an unpleasant surprise.

9...e5?!
More critical, of course, is 9...♗xc3 10.bxc3 (in this way the bishop gains access to the a3-square, and the rook will be able to create pressure on the b-file; in the event of 10.dxc3 ♘xe4 11.♗d3 f5 Black is alright) 10...♘xe4 11.♖b1 or 11.♗a3!? – White has an active game, but a pawn is a pawn.

10.♕g3 dxe4
In the source game Bacrot-Zelcic (Zagreb 2018) 10...0-0 11.d3 ♕d6

12.exd5 cxd5 13.♘b5 was tried, with the initiative for White.

11.d3 exd3 12.♗xd3 ♘bd7

13.♘e2?!
The straightforward 13.♕xg7 ♖g8 14.♕h6 with the threats of ♗f5 and ♗g5 would appear to be stronger – the black king will not feel safe either in the centre, or on the queenside. An important nuance: if 14...♕b6, White replies 15.♗f5!, ignoring the threat to the f2-pawn, when it would appear that Black's position collapses.

13...0-0? Now Black becomes the co-author of an opening catastrophe. 13...♗b6! was correct, and after 14.♕xg7 ♖g8 15.♕h6 he has 15...e4!

16.♗c4 ♕e7 with counter-chances – his king can hide on the queenside.

14.♗f5 Now the white bishops become a powerful force, whereas the black bishop, by contrast, becomes a target for attack.

14...♘c5? The decisive mistake, after which the centralized bishop loses all its retreat squares. It was possible to defend after 14...♖e8 15.c3 ♗c5 16.♗g5 ♕c7 17.♕h4 h6!? 18.♗xh6 ♘f8, and if 19.♕g5, then 19...♘e6. Of course, this entire defensive construction looks suspicious, but here, at least, Black does not lose immediately.

15.♗h6 ♘h5 Black is also lost after 15...♘e6 16.♗xe6 ♘h5 17.♕g4 fxe6

Maxime Vachier-Lagrave reached the final of the Riga Grand Prix in a most efficient manner, without a single tiebreak.

18.♕xe6+ ♔h8 19.♗e3. **16.♕g4 ♕d6 17.♕xh5 ♕xh6 18.♕xh6 gxh6 19.c3** Black resigned.

In the return encounter MVL confidently defended the black pieces and qualified for the quarter final. Shakhriyar Mamedyarov also achieved his objective in 'normal time': his opponent Daniil Dubov both times played the opening very interestingly (this is in general his 'hobby'), but in the second game he failed to control things at a later stage.

So, the main heroes of the Riga stage, MVL and Shakh, immediately showed that they were in good form, but in all the other matches tie-breaks were required. In the following rapid game White succeeded with a spectacular attack.

Alexander Grischuk
Nikita Vitiugov
Riga 2019 (1.3)

position after 16.e4

Alexander Grischuk is one of those who constantly and very successfully carry out research work in the opening, regularly bemusing his opponents with new ideas. In one of the lines of the Queen's Gambit White has sacrificed a pawn, gaining compensation in the form of a strong centre and a lead in development. It is clear that Black must somehow complete his development and shelter his king, but how? It is not easy to decide on 16...0-0 in view of the threats of e5 and ♗h4 with ♘g5, in one order or another. Needless to say, the computer easily defends itself in all lines, but Nikita took an understandably human decision: to wait a little, and for the moment not determine the position of the king.

16...♗c7 17.♗h4 ♕d7 17...f6!? deserved attention, with the idea of 18.e5 0-0 19.exf6 gxf6 20.♖d1 ♕e8!? (if 20...♔h8, then 21.♘e5 ♕e8 22.♖h3!? looks threatening).
18.♖d1 0-0? Inconsistent, to say the least – Black castles at the most inappropriate moment. It was possible to hold on after 18...f6 19.♘e5 ♕e7 20.♘c4 (20.♕h5+ g6) 20...b5!? 21.♘e5 0-0, when the pawn on c6 cannot be captured because of 22..♕d6.
19.♘e5 ♕e8

20.♗f6! A combination, as though taken from the pages of a school chess manual! **20...♖d8** Or 20...gxf6 21.♕h5 with mate in a few moves. **21.♗xg7 ♔xg7 22.♖g3+ ♔h8 23.♕h5** Black resigned.

Hikaru Nakamura was apparently so sure about his superiority over Veselin Topalov in rapid chess, that he did not especially exert himself at the classic time rate. However, the former World Champion reminded his younger opponent that he himself also plays rapid quite well. With White in an anti-Marshall he did not simply outplay, but practically stalemated Black, and in an already hopeless position Nakamura blundered a knight.
Also in two rapid games the young Polish grandmaster Jan-Krzysztof Duda defeated eight-time Russian champion Peter Svidler, and Wesley So overcame Pentala Harikrishna.

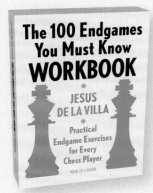

Epic tiebreaks

The two remaining matches, Karjakin-Giri and Yu Yangyi-Aronian, went to an Armageddon. As Anish Giri wrote on Twitter, 'Fought hard, but despite all our efforts with @SergeyKaryakin it seems we still didn't manage to play the most epic tiebreak of the day. #RigaGP#Wimbledon'. Indeed, the tiebreak between Djokovic and Federer at Wimbledon was unforgettable. But also Levon Aronian and Yu Yangyi fought desperately in the first round. In the Armageddon Aronian gained a promising position with White, but was unable to convert his advantage. A 4½-4½ draw in the match, and the Chinese player went through to the quarter final.

Let us nevertheless take a look at an extract from the gripping match between the Russian and Dutch grandmasters.

Anish Giri
Sergey Karjakin
Riga 2019 (tiebreak-6)

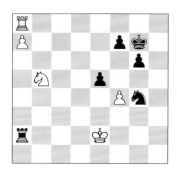

position after 37...♖a2

Just one accurate king move separated Anish from progressing to the next round. After 38.♔d3 ♘f2+ 39.♔c3 the checks would have come to an end, and Black would have had to give up his rook for the passed a7-pawn.
However, in time-trouble one purely instinctively wants, as a rule, to make some forcing move, to create a threat or attack something, and Giri played: **38.♔f3?** In reply there immediately followed **38...f5!**

It is not just that the knight is defended, but 39...e4+ 40.♔g3 ♘e3 is also threatened, with mate in a few moves. White was forced to exchange, **39.fxe5**, but after **39...♘xe5+ 40.♔f4 ♘c6** the knight joined the defence in time, and soon a draw was agreed.
In the Armageddon Giri, with Black, made an 'unforced error' in a comparatively quiet and roughly equal position when he voluntarily weakened his king. Obtaining a clear target to attack, Karjakin cut through Black's defences in a few moves.

Quarter final

In the quarter final only Vachier-Lagrave achieved his objective in normal time. In the first game Topalov, playing White, decided to join battle in the main lines of the Najdorf Variation. This idea proved not very successful: MVL was clearly not inferior to his more experienced opponent in knowledge, and at the same time he was obviously more in practice, and superior in the calcu-

FIDE GP 2019 – standings				
		1	**2**	**total**
1	Shakhriyar Mamedyarov	0	10	10
2	Alexander Grischuk	7	3	10
3	Ian Nepomniachtchi	9		9
4	Maxime Vachier-Lagrave		8	8
5	Radoslaw Wojtaszek	5		5
6	Wesley So	1	3	4
7	Hikaru Nakamura	3	0	3
8-9	Peter Svidler	2	0	2
	Daniil Dubov	2	0	2
10	Wei Yi	2		2
11	Jan-Krzysztof Duda	0	1	1
12	Sergey Karjakin	0	1	1
13	Yu Yangyi		1	1
14	Veselin Topalov		1	1
15-21	Anish Giri	0	0	0
	Levon Aronian	0	0	0
	Nikita Vitiugov	0	0	0
	Teimour Radjabov	0		0
	Pentala Harikrishna		0	0
	David Navara	0		0
	Dmitry Jakovenko	0		0

1=Moscow; 2=Riga (To play: Hamburg and Tel Aviv)

lation of variations and resourcefulness. Commenting on the game afterwards in the press conference, the former World Champion looked extremely disillusioned with his play. In the return game he obtained a dubious position with Black and already on emerging from the opening he offered a draw.

Grischuk and Mamedyarov quite confidently overcame their opponents in 25-minute games, while with So and Karjakin things went to blitz, where Sergey caught out his opponent in the opening.

Wesley So
Sergey Karjakin
Riga 2019 (tiebreak-5)
English Opening, Four Knights Variation
1.c4 ♘f6 2.♘c3 e5 3.♘f3 ♘c6 4.g3 ♗b4 5.♗g2 0-0 6.♘d5 ♗c5 7.0-0 d6 8.e3 ♖e8 9.d4

All the preceding games had ended in a draw, and were not especially prolonged. The American grandmaster decided to change the opening tune, and instead of 1.d4 or 1.e4 (where Karjakin had confidently equalized) he went into an English Opening. But here also Sergey was well prepared.
9...♗g4! 10.dxc5 e4 11.♘c3?
The correct move 11.h3 was tested in the game Nepomniachtchi-Vitiugov, Satka 2018.
11...♘e5!
Black fully exploits all the benefits of the pin. Now 12.♘xe4 ♘xe4 13.h3 ♘xf3+ 14.♗xf3 ♗xh3 is cheerless for White, but Wesley So is justly famed for his resourcefulness.

12.♘xe5! ♗xd1 13.♘xf7 ♕e7
An accurate move, but it took Sergey a whole minute, if not more.
14.♘xd6 cxd6 15.cxd6 ♕xd6 16.♖xd1 ♕e5

White has two bishops and two pawns for the queen, so that nominally he is only one pawn down. But all the black pieces are very active, and the queen is strong.
17.♗d2 ♖ad8 18.♗e1 b6 19.b3 ♖d3 20.♖xd3 exd3 21.♖d1 ♖d8 22.♗f1 ♕f5
I have practically no doubt that after 22...d2!? 23.♖xd2 ♖xd2 24.♗xd2 ♘e4 25.♘xe4 ♕xe4 Karjakin with his technique would have converted the advantage into a win.
23.♘d5! ♘xd5 24.♖xd3 ♔f8 25.cxd5

It is very probable that initially Karjakin was intending to capture the pawn with 25...♖xd5?, but at the last moment he noticed 26.♗b4+ ♔e8 27.e4! ♕xe4 28.♖e3. He had to switch to defence, and first Black restricts the dark-squared bishop.
25...a5 26.♖d4 ♕b1 27.♗c3 ♕xa2 28.♗c4 ♕c2 29.♖f4+ ♔e7 30.♗xg7

Wesley So with a local fan. The American's tournament ended in the semi-finals when he was knocked out by Shakhriyar Mamedyarov.

30...♖d6?
The decisive mistake. Black overlooked that a convenient opportunity to capture the powerful passed pawn had presented itself – 30...♖xd5!, when in the event of 31.♗xd5 ♕d1+ 32.♔g2 ♕xd5+ and 33... ♕xb3 Black is again playing for a win. Stronger is 31.e4! ♖h5!? 32.♗f6+ ♔d7; the computer produces '0.00', but it is a crazy position, with three results possible. Now, however, it all concludes quickly.
31.♗f8+ ♔d7 32.♗b5+ ♔c7 33.♖c4+
Black resigned.

In the return blitz game the scenario was almost exactly repeated the other way round, but this 'almost' decided the fate of the qualification to the semi-final. Karjakin played the opening badly and was a pawn down in a difficult position. But he began 'clinging to life', seeking the slightest chances, and So faltered: after several inaccuracies it was his position that was now hopeless. Nevertheless, Sergey was the last to go wrong in this topsy-turvy tie-break, and Wesley escaped to a draw by perpetual check.

Semi-final
Surprisingly enough, in neither of the matches was a tie-break required, thanks to which the winners gained two whole free days before the final encounter.

Shakh Mamedyarov's win against Wesley So was a typical example of modern opening battles: White requested his opponent to 'present his documents' in one of the forcing theoretical lines with a slight deviation from the well-trodden theoretical paths. If Black had known (or found at the board) the correct continuation, it would have immediately resulted in a draw. Mamedyarov pointed out the correct path immediately after the game – there was no point in concealing it, as anyone with a computer would immediately discover what was what anyway. But at the board So was unable to solve the problem.

Shakhriyar Mamedyarov
Wesley So
Riga 2019 (3.1)
Catalan Opening, Open Variation

1.d4 ♘f6 2.c4 e6 3.♘f3 d5 4.g3 ♗e7 5.♗g2 0-0 6.0-0 dxc4 7.♘e5 ♘c6 8.♘xc6 bxc6 9.♘a3 ♗xa3 10.bxa3 ♗a6 11.♕d2 ♖b8 12.♕a5 ♖b6 13.a4 ♕d6

14.a3!?
A novelty; previously White had tried 14.e4 ♕b4! 15.♕xb4 ♖xb4 16.♗a3 ♖xa4 17.♗xf8 ♔xf8, with compensation for the exchange. With the move in the game White covers the b4-square, thereby avoiding the queen exchange.
14...♖fb8 15.e4

Black has been set a specific question, and what should be the answer (or more precisely, two answers) was given by Mamedyarov himself:
A) 15...♕d8 16.♖d1 (White wants to place his bishop on b4, but after the immediate 16.♗d2? Black has 16...c3) 16...♕c8 17.♗d2 ♖b3 18.♗b4 ♕b7.
B) It is also possible to sacrifice the exchange: 15...♘xe4!? 16.♗xe4 ♕xd4 17.♗e3 ♕xe4 18.♗xb6 ♖xb6.
Wesley So spent a lot of time here (according to Mamedyarov, he even criticized his move 14...♖fb8, although it is quite normal) and he decided to give up two pieces for a rook and pawn. An emotional decision – soon it transpired that the position had become a technical one, so strong were the white bishops.
15...c3 16.e5 ♕d8
16...♕xd4 17.♗e3 ♕d3 18.exf6 ♖b1 19.♕g5 was also bad. Another hypothesis – in his calculation of the line 16...♕d8 17.exf6 ♗xf1 18.♗xf1 c2 Wesley overlooked White's reply 19.♖a2.
17.exf6 ♗xf1 18.♗xf1 c2

19.♖a2! An accurate move: White not only picks up the dangerous passed pawn, but also removes all threats on the back rank.
19...♕d5 20.♕xd5 cxd5 21.♖xc2 gxf6 22.♖xc7 ♖8b7 23.♖c5 ♔g7 24.♔g2 ♖b1 25.♗b5 ♖a1 26.♖c3 ♖b6 27.♗f4 ♖b7 28.♔f3 ♖d1 29.♗e3 ♖b1 30.♔g4 ♖h1 31.h4 ♔g6 32.♗d3+ f5+ 33.♔f3 ♖d1 34.g4
Black resigned.
    In the return game Shakhriyar confidently made a draw with Black.

Game of the tournament
Maxime Vachier-Lagrave, by contrast, began with a draw against Alexander Grischuk, but on the second day he won with Black, and in brilliant style. To my mind, this was the game of the tournament.

**NOTES BY
Anish Giri**

Alexander Grischuk
Maxime Vachier-Lagrave
Riga 2019 (3.2)
King's Indian Defence

1.d4 ♘f6 2.c4 g6 3.h4!?

This line is not exactly new. In fact, it has been around for a while and even I had the honour to play against it in the 2016 Moscow Candidates tournament, courtesy of Veselin Topalov. I thought it couldn't be good back then, but times are changing and now the top players are much more open-minded and generally more patient when it comes to questioning established dogmas.
The idea is obviously aimed at the Grünfeld Defence, and the main point is that after 3...♗g7 4.♘c3 d5 White has 5.h5!, which is a funny reversed version of the rule that an attack on the flank must be met with a strike in the centre. In fact, that is exactly how a game Grischuk-Nepomniachtchi in the Levitov Chess Week in Amsterdam went.
3...c5 4.d5 b5
Going for a Benko Gambit reply is also how I reacted to the premature-

looking Harry-the-h-pawn push. It turns out that things are not so simple, however, and it may not even be the best way to fight h4 at all.
5.cxb5 a6

6.e3!
Topalov obediently captured on a6, which did indeed lead to a fantastic Benko. Here White can develop a lot more freely. In fact, this is also a big system without the inclusion of the moves ...g6 and h4.
6...♗g7 7.♘c3 0-0 8.♘f3 d6
It was worth considering something more energetic, connected with ...e6!?.
9.a4! ♗g4!?

The most logical move in the position, but not a top choice of the engine, which is why Alexander Grischuk was on his own from here on in.
10.♖a3
10.e4!? also made sense. Note that White is obviously postponing the development of the f1-bishop, so that he can capture on b5 in one go.
10...axb5
Black runs out of useful moves, while White still has e3-e4 in reserve. So he decides to capture after all.
11.♗xb5 ♘a6 12.e4 ♘b4
It was also interesting to send this knight elsewhere, for example to c7 or maybe to b6 via d7. Many options.
13.♗e2

13...♘d7 I strongly disliked the look of this move, as I thought that in this particular Benko structure with the h-pawn on h4 it is more sensible to guard against the potential h5 push (after the light-squared bishops get traded), but on the other hand Black really needs to generate some play of his own, so this common knight manoeuvre does make sense. The only other sensible plan would probably be connected with ...e7-e6.
14.0-0 ♕b6 I am not sure what Black wants exactly, but one of his ideas is to try to establish a knight on d3 in the future and keep the ...f7-f5 break in mind. In the game it all works out perfectly, but at this point I wasn't so sure that Maxime Vachier-Lagrave was doing the right thing.

15.♖e1?!
A terrible move in hindsight, because the rook simply goes back to f1 later in the game, away from a potential ...♘d3. The computer likes 15.♘b5!?, clearing the third rank for the rook and keeping ♘g5 in reserve.
I also quite like the immediate 15.♘g5!?, when after 15...♗xe2 16.♕xe2 Black is yet to prove his compensation, while the h4-pawn no

ALPHAZERO DRAMATICALLY CHANGED HARRY THE H-PAWN'S LIFE

longer seems awkward, now that h4-h5 may be on the agenda.

15...♕b7 16.♗g5 ♗xf3

With the rook on e1, this idea is particularly attractive. The knights are heading towards the d3-square.

Alexander Grischuk was deeply impressed by the masterful play of Maxime Vachier-Lagrave in what turned out to be the game of the tournament.

17.gxf3!? This saves White some time (he doesn't have to withdraw the bishop to e2), but ruining the pawn structure this way is very courageous. 17.♗xf3 ♘e5 18.♗e2 c4 19.♕d2 ♘bd3 20.♖b1 f5 gives Black good counter-play, but after 21.exf5 gxf5 22.♗f4 White will manage to get rid of the d3-knight and keep things well under control.

17...♘e5 18.♖f1!? 18.♘a2!? was also possible, which would be another way of stopping the ...c4/...♘d3 idea.

18...c4 The promised ...♘d3 idea is becoming as real as ever.

18...f5 is met nicely by 19.f4.

19.b3 ♖fc8 Keeping the tension is a good practical decision. 19...♘xf3+ 20.♗xf3 ♗xc3 21.bxc4 ♘e5 22.♔g2 would give White an easy life.

20.♗d2?!

It's hard to blame White for not seeing 10 strong moves ahead, but now things start getting out of hand, as MVL starts

pulling French rabbits out of his hat. There was actually no threat to the c3-knight, so the real prophylactic move was 20.♔g2!, when Black wouldn't have his tactics working so nicely for him as in the game.

20...♘bd3! 21.f4 ♕b4! 22.♘b1 c3 Tempo play by Maxime; le move by move! **23.fxe5 ♘b2!** Machine! **24.♕c2 cxd2 25.♕xb2 ♕xe4! 26.♕xd2 ♖c2**

A very powerful tactical sequence is coming to an end, and it now appears that White is losing back the piece and has to fight for survival in an ugly endgame.

27.♕d3 ♖xe2 28.♕xe4 ♖xe4 29.exd6 exd6 30.♘d2 ♖g4+ 31.♔h1 ♖xh4+ 32.♔g2 ♖d4! 33.♘f3 ♖g4+! 34.♔h3 ♖b4!

Black has to balance monitoring White's queenside pawns and thinking of his own plans on the kingside. So far Maxime is doing it very well, as the knight on f3 is clearly misplaced now and can't assist on the queenside.

35.♖b1 ♖c8?!

This doesn't exactly work, because of a very beautiful saving resource that both sides missed. 35...♗c3! is the machine's choice.

36.♔g2 ♖c3

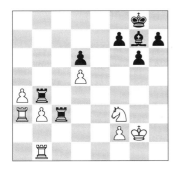

37.♘g1? The normal defence, since it seemed that ...♖g4+ was going to win Black a piece, but it turns out White had a path to salvation. White should have put more faith in his queenside pawns!

After 37.♖e1!! ♖g4+ (if Black doesn't pick up the knight, White will play ♖e3) 38.♔f1 ♖xf3 39.♖e8+ ♗f8 White has given up a piece, but now it turns out that his slow but determined a-passer will just make it in time to the other side: 40.a5! ♖b4 41.a6, and Black has nothing better than giving up a rook for the pawn, with a draw.

37...♖c2 38.♘f3 ♖g4+ 39.♔f1 ♖f4 40.♔g2 ♖g4+ 41.♔f1 ♖f4 42.♔g2 g5! Here it turns out that the a-pawn is actually not in time. Compared to the other line, White still has his knight on the board, but Black's rooks are x-raying the f2-pawn and once it falls, checkmate is near.

43.♖f1 43.a5 g4 44.a6 ♖xf3 45.a7 ♖fxf2+, and Black will mate, since the g7-bishop will join in as well.

43...♖g4+ 44.♔h1

44.♔h3 was a better attempt to keep things going, but objectively speaking, White is already losing.

44...♖c3! 45.♖g1

45...♖f4!

Maxime masterfully manoeuvres his heavy artillery. White's king is in a kind of a mating net, being under the crossfire of the black rooks.

46.♘h2 46.♘xg5 would actually lose to the simple 46...h6, when the knight is trapped.

46...♖xf2 47.♖xg5 ♖cc2

And White resigned, as there is no stopping the mate. Bravo!

■ ■ ■

Quite an incredible course

Before the final between Mamedyarov and Vachier-Lagrave, their score in classical chess was an impressive 6-1 (not counting draws) in Mamedyarov's favour. In rapid and blitz the score was roughly equal. But soon all these computations and forecasts had to be forgotten as the match took a quite incredible course. At the start, employing a new idea in the Grünfeld Defence, Shakh won in three hours and 28 moves.

NOTES BY
Anish Giri

Shakhriyar Mamedyarov
Maxime Vachier-Lagrave
Riga 2019 (20)
Grünfeld Indian, Exchange Variation

1.d4 ♘f6 2.c4 g6 3.♘c3 d5 4.cxd5 ♘xd5 5.e4 ♘xc3 6.bxc3 ♗g7 7.♕a4+

There are plenty of different systems against the Grünfeld, and most of them are pretty critical. I guess this is one of the few reasons that this other-wise excellent dynamic opening for Black has not been all that popular at the highest level recently.

7...♕d7

7...♘d7 is an altogether different approach, but apart from some blitz games in his online match against Nakamura, Vachier-Lagrave has remained faithful to the queen move.

8.♕a3 In the last encounter between the same players in this position, St. Louis 2016, Mamedyarov tried 8.♗b5, with an eventual draw.

8...b6 9.♘f3 ♗b7 10.♗d3 0-0 11.0-0 c5 12.♗f4!?

A new move. Suddenly Black's position is very critical. Bogner played 12.♖d1 against MVL in 2015, worrying about the d4-pawn.

12...cxd4 13.cxd4 ♘c6?
As Black, you should generally try not to end up in a situation like this, when your only move is a risky pawn-grabbing adventure giving up the vital g7-bishop. That said, once you land in such a situation, you do usually have to go for it.

Black had to take the pawn, 13...♗xd4 14.♘xd4 ♕xd4, when White can choose to play for positional compensation, or force matters with 15.♕xe7, when stuff gets traded and Black gets good drawing chances due to the limited material: 15.♕xe7 ♕xd3 16.♕xb7 ♘d7 17.♖fd1 ♘c5. The endgame after the queens have left the board is for two results only, but it was better than the game anyway.
14.d5

14...♘a5? This is already the second game that I annotate in this issue in which MVL has a knight out of play on a5 and eventually lets the d-pawn queen. On the other hand, that's the downside of the Grünfeld. Of course, in a parallel universe Maxime probably managed to get the knight to c4, to control the c-file and to eventually capture the d5-pawn, which, by the way, is exactly what happened in his game against Hikaru Nakamura in the London GCT last year. After 14...♘d4 15.♘xd4 ♗xd4 Black at least doesn't have to deal with 'knight-on-the-rim' issues.

15.♖ac1 ♖fc8 16.h3 Black's only idea appears to be to challenge the d5-pawn with ...e6, and after d6 try to isolate it with ...f6, but Shakh notices that he has a strong antidote and just makes a useful waiting move.

16.h4! is a little more 2019, but the game move is very efficient, too.

16...e6 17.d6 f6

18.e5! A strong reply, not allowing Black to go ...e5, when he would have hopes of eventually gobbling up the d6-pawn. **18...♗xf3 19.exf6!** Intermezzo! **19...♗xf6 20.gxf3 e5 21.♗d2!**

The h3-pawn is completely irrelevant, while the white bishops are raging.

21...♖xc1 After 21...♕xh3 22.♗e4! the chances of a perpetual remain zero, despite Black picking up the h3-pawn and coming close with his queen.

22.♖xc1 ♖c8

The trade of rooks doesn't help much, since Black will not be in time to surround the d6-pawn and his knight will never get into play.

23.♖xc8+ ♕xc8 24.♔g2 ♗d8

25.♗e4! White's bishop is dominating the knight, because 25...♘c4 fails due to 26.♗d5+, followed by 27.♕xa7+ or 27.d7.

25...♕e6 26.♕d3 ♔g7 27.♗c3 ♕f6 28.♔f1

Black has no moves at all and the e5-pawn is doomed to fall. With no perpetual in sight either and realizing how hopeless his situation is, he just resigned.

■ ■ ■

The next day, when the Frenchman needed to win 'to order', he chose a quiet variation of the Italian Game. On the emergence from the opening the position looked absolutely equal and 'empty', but MVL showed that he

Shakhriyar Mamedyarov seemed to be in clover after he won the first classical game in the final, but it was only in the Armageddon game that he decided the Riga GP in his favour.

is an excellent psychologist: Mamedyarov is not able to play for a draw, and the situation was uncomfortable for him. The Azeri grandmaster embarked on some strange queen manoeuvres, left his king without defenders, and succumbed to an irresistible attack. In order to gain revenge, Maxime needed the same three hours and practically the same number of moves – 32.

In the tiebreak the most gripping events occurred in the blitz and the Armageddon. After four draws Shakh again moved ahead, winning with Black. Again he needed only a draw, and with the white pieces. But an attempt to force himself to play reservedly did not succeed: not avoiding exchanges and simplification, MVL managed to seize the initiative in the endgame, win a pawn and convert his advantage.

Armageddon! Shakh was given Black, and again he would be satisfied with a draw... But here he acted very wisely: forgetting what result satisfied him, he went in for a grand battle, choosing the King's Indian

Defence. In an open struggle Mamedyarov felt in his element! Objectively, White evidently gained the better chances from the opening, but in such a nervy situation this did not have particular significance: it was far more important that the pieces 'jumped' around the board, and the scene of battle constantly changed. Finally, in a dynamically balanced position White had to avoid a repetition of moves, but then the scales tipped in Black's favour – Shakhriyar converted his advantage into a win.

At the final press conference Shakhriyar Mamedyarov emphasized that Maxime Vachier-Lagrave conducted the Riga stage very strongly, winning all his matches in normal time. But when things came to the tie-break, he was less prepared than his opponent, who had already played a tie-break. And he remembered the knock-out World Championship in Libya in 2004, where Veselin crushed everyone in his path in 'normal time', but in the semifinal he stumbled in his very first tie-break. ■

Judit Polgar

Professional blunders

Blunders used to be really gross mistakes, but these days the use of the word is much farther-ranging. **JUDIT POLGAR** takes a look at high-level blunders that every player can draw lessons from.

Although it's frequently used in chess folklore, the term 'blunder' does not have a clear meaning. Nowadays, many players use it for any weak move. Yet it feels more accurate to associate it with tactical oversights, which can occur in various different circumstances. A player's strength also makes a difference – a blunder at 2700+ level and one in a beginner's game do not look the same.

In this article, I have further restricted the meaning by mainly referring to moments at which very strong players, immersed in deep strategic planning, overlook a simple and concrete detail early in their main variations.

This makes things more interesting, because even when 'blundering' a small (or not so small) amount of material in one or two moves, the correctness of a player's strategic approach at least partly compensates for the damage done and keeps the game alive.

And if the 'blundering' player keeps his composure and focus in what follows, the final result may still be a happy one (or, at a superficial level, a lucky one).

For mere mortals, the fact that not even World Champions are immune to blundering must be refreshing and encouraging.

Magnus Carlsen
Gawain Jones
Wijk aan Zee 2018

position after 16...♗c8

In this typical Sicilian Dragon, White has the better queenside structure and the safer king, but Black's kingside majority may be threatening in the long run. White's general plan is directed precisely against this compact structure, which he should undermine with h2-h4-h5 and g2-g4, not only securing squares for his minor pieces, but also opening files for an attack.

17.g4?? Carlsen had obviously intended this as a pawn sacrifice, aimed at either opening the f-file for his attack, or yielding him the e4-square for the knight.

The correct way of starting the attack was 17.h4, over-defending the knight and getting ready for h4-h5.

17...f4! Despite the favourable result of the game, there is no doubt that while dreaming of the light squares, Magnus had overlooked this simple move, winning a piece.

His main line might have been 17...fxg4 18.h4 gxh3 19.♘xh3, with excellent attacking chances for the pawn.

18.h4 fxe3 19.♕xe3

The remarkable thing is that the World Champion continued as if nothing serious had happened, and there actually are some good reasons for this. After all, White has got what he

For mere mortals, the fact that not even World Champions are immune to blundering must be encouraging.

wanted: the e4-square and the better structure all over the board. From a practical point of view, Black is still far from winning, even though objectively speaking there is no doubt about the evaluation of the position. Also, even a strong grandmaster like Jones must have found it hard to control his euphoria after winning a piece for a pawn and may have felt that it was only a matter of time before White would resign.

19...h6 20.♕c5 ♗b7 21.♘e4 ♖e6 22.h5

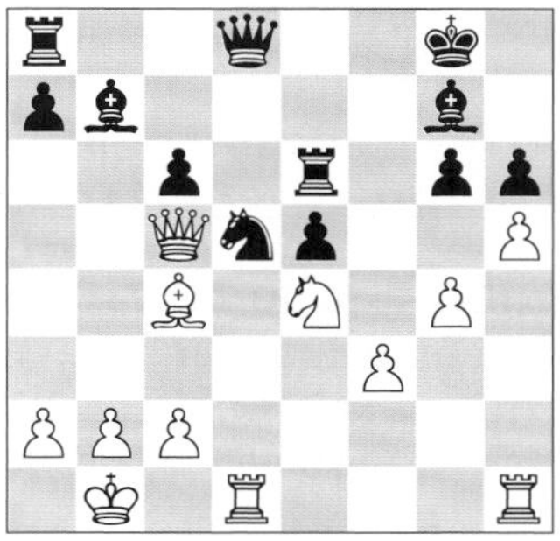

22...♕b6? There is this general rule that the player with a material advantage should exchange pieces (especially queens). But this move is a clear sign of lack of patience. First of all, 23...♕xc5 is not a threat, as after 24.♘xc5 ♖e7 25.♘xb7 ♖xb7 26.♖xd5 White retrieves the material with interest.

Secondly, it is always a good idea to keep your king safe, which suggests 22...g5 as the simplest way to consolidate Black's advantage.

23.g5! Carlsen immediately uses his chance, continuing the main plan initiated by his blunder.

23...hxg5 24.♕a3 The position has turned unclear already and White went on to win against a probably demoralized opponent.

Apart from the psychological aspects involving Carlsen's composure and Jones's emotions, the objective factor allowing this miracle to happen was the soundness of the strategic concept connected with the e4-square and the opening of the kingside files.

There are also cases in which a player can commit an apparent blunder based on subconscious elements, as in the next example.

Shakhriyar Mamedyarov
Alexander Grischuk
Stavanger 2019

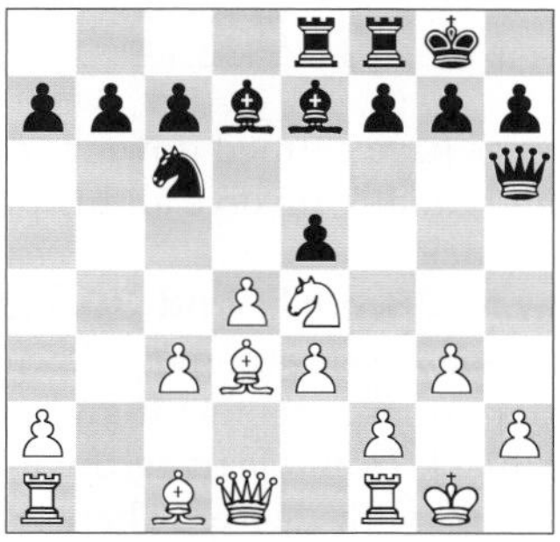

position after 13...♗e7

White's opening play had been strategically ambitious, aimed at gaining space and putting the enemy queen in an uncomfortable situation.

14.f4 f5 I was a commentator at this prestigious event and when, right after the game, I respectfully praised Grischuk for his interesting pawn sacrifice, I was surprised when he answered that it had in fact been a blunder!

He must have been reluctant to release the tension with 14...exd4 15.exd4 (threatening f5) 15...♗f5 16.♖b1!. Now the main threat is 17.♖b5, playing against the blocking bishop, since 17.♖xb7 would run into 17...♘xd4, followed by the double attack 18...♕c6. But later the pawn will be really hanging, causing Black to lose a tempo. 16...a6 17.♘f2 ♗xd3 18.♕xd3 ♘a5 19.f5, with an initiative for White.

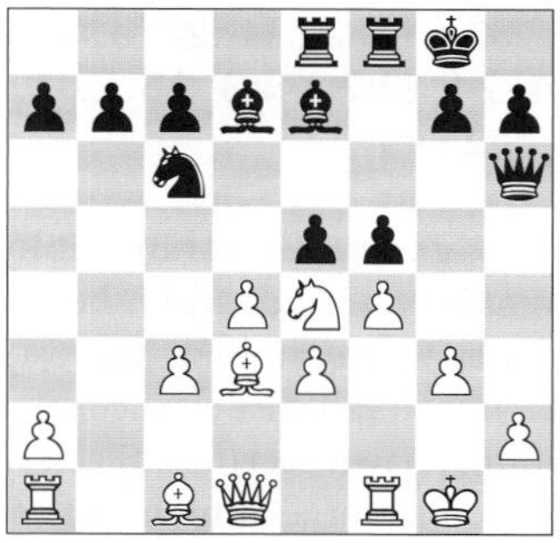

15.♗c4+ Grischuk blundered this move order, as he had calculated the capture on e5 only with the move order 15.dxe5? fxe4 16.♗c4+ ♗e6, with an extra piece for Black.

15...♔h8 15...♗e6 is not indicated now: 16.♗xe6+ ♕xe6 17.d5 ♕f7 18.dxc6 fxe4 19.cxb7, destroying Black's queenside and giving White an edge.

16.dxe5

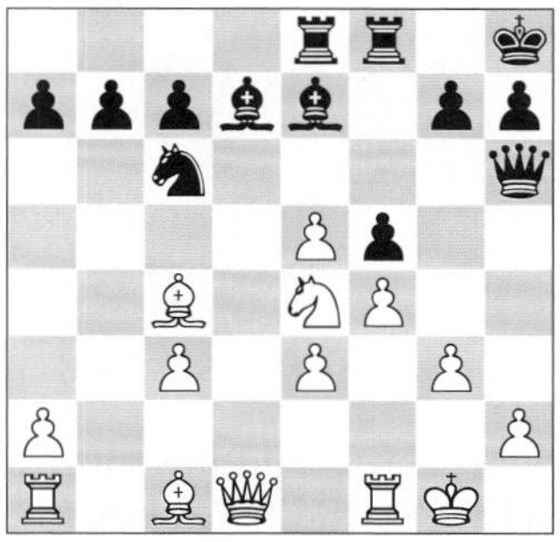

Even though he had not anticipated this course of events, Black has got what he wanted: the bishop on c1 is passive and far from finding a decent way to develop. After a few precise moves, Black's compensation will be obvious.

16...♖d8! 17.♘f2 ♘a5 18.♗d3

18.♗e2 is too passive, allowing Black to build up dangerous counterplay: 18...♗c6 19.♕c2 g5. After ...gxf4 exf4, the dark-squared bishop could join its colleague for the attack with ...♗c5, with threats like ...♕h3 or ...♖g8xg3+, followed by ...♕h1, mate.

18...♗b5 19.♕c2 ♗xd3 20.♘xd3 ♕c6

Black's control of the light squares and the passive bishop on c1 offer entirely adequate compensation.

21.♘b2 ♘c4 22.♕e2 ♘a3 23.♘d1 ♘c4 24.♘b2 ♘a3 25.♘d1 ♘c4 26.♘b2 Draw.

In this game, Grischuk's blunder was entirely 'sound' and if he had not confessed to overlooking the best move order, it would have been accepted as a positional pawn sacrifice. Black simply achieved his initial aim: that of keeping the bishop on c1 passive.

But in the next game the blunder needed a radical plan to readjust to the situation.

Magnus Carlsen
Richard Rapport
Wijk aan Zee 2019

position after 24...♖fe8

White is active and has more space. With his next move, Carlsen intended to win the pawn on d6, based on the pin along the d-file.

25.e5! ♗xg2 26.♕xg2

Magnus later confessed that he had overlooked that the bishop exchange would force him to release the pressure along the d-file. But his better coordination allowed him to start a very strong attack, more than compensating the 'sacrificed' pawn.

26...dxe5 27.♘d5 e4 The best practical chance. Black tries to keep the position as closed as possible. The alternatives lead to earlier problems than the game continuation.

If 27...exf4, the least White can do is winning an exchange with 28.♗c7, as any rook move would lose the queen to 29.♘xe7+.

While Rapport was thinking, Carlsen worked out the following line:

27...♗d6 28.♘c7 ♗xc7 29.♕xb7 ♖xb7 30.♖xd7 ♖c8 31.fxe5, when the reserve rook would soon join the battle along the f-file, winning at least an exchange. These kinds of variations convinced Magnus that everything was working out well for him after his blunder and restored his confidence.

28.♗c3

Things have calmed down and White can gradually involve all his pieces in the attack.

28...f6 29.♔h1 ♔h8 30.♖g1 ♗f8 31.♘e3 An elegant move, keeping the attacking process fluent and preventing Black from clearing the e-file for his rooks with ...e4-e3. There is little to comment on in this phase, as White's pieces flow naturally towards the enemy king, clearing squares for each other on the way.

31...♕c6 32.♖d5 ♕e6 33.♖h5

Another elegant manoeuvre. The rook has done a good job along the d-file after the blunder/combination, but now displays its horizontal mobility to join the kingside attack.

33...♕f7 34.♕h3 g6

Or if 34...h6 then 35.♘f5 ♖b7 36.♖h4, followed by ♖hg4. The knight sacrifice

on h6 is also an issue, but White would do better to keep it in reserve.

35.♖h4 ♖b6 36.f5

After the rook has reached the h-file, White can use the squares along the fifth rank for his pawn and knight.

36...♘e5 37.♘d5 ♖d6 37...g5 leads to a more prosaic win: 38.♖xe4 ♘c6 39.♗xe5 ♖xe5 40.♖xe5 fxe5 41.♖xg5, when White has won a pawn and retains a huge strategic advantage.

38.fxg6 The start of a small combination. **38...♘xg6**

39.♗xf6+! ♖xf6 40.♖xh7+!

Black resigned. After 40...♕xh7 41.♕xh7+ ♔xh7 42.♘xf6+ White wins an exchange and the game.

Carlsen's convincing win after the blunder was possible due to his re-assessment of his strategic pluses and his ability to put all the puzzle pieces into the right place.

Conclusion

■ When designing deep strategic plans, or even simple concrete operations, always double-check whether your opponent can go for an early deviation.

■ If you have nevertheless blundered, take a fresh look at the position and re-assess it without thinking of the previous phase. There could be elements offering you compensation, either along the lines of your original plan, or based on new ideas.

■ There are cases when your blunder is not really a blunder, so it is useful to give some credit to your subconscious.

■ But above all, do not lose faith and composure after blundering! ■

MAXIMize your Tactics Solutions

1. Bu Xiangzhi-Jones
Hengshui (rapid) 2019

32...♘f3+! Since 33.♕xf3 loses to 33...♖xe1+ White has to give the black major pieces access to the vital squares and lines: **33.gxf3 ♖g5+ 34.♔f1 ♕h3+ 35.♔e2 ♖g2** And Black easily converted.

2. Roseneck-Krassowizkij
Magdeburg 2019

24.♖7d6! Black resigned. If the queen retreats White wins the exchange with 25.♘f6+ while if he accepts the sacrifice Black sustains even heavier losses, the key line being 24...♗xd6 25.cxd6 ♖d7 26.♘c5 ♕f5 27.g4.

3. Schekachikhin-Matlakov
Sochi 2019

34.♖xh7+! Black resigned as he is either checkmated or has to give up the queen: 34...♕xh7 35.♕e8+ ♔g8 36.♖h1 mate or 34...♔xh7 35.♖h1+ ♔g8 36.♕xd5+ ♔f7 (36...♔f8 37.♖h8+) 37.♘h6+.

4. Moradiabadi-Neiksans
St. Louis 2019

White lost after 42.g4? hxg4+ 43.♔g3 ♖d2 44.♖g8+ ♔f5. He could have held with **42.♖g8+! ♔f5 43.♖xg5+! ♔xg5 44.♗c7!** when Black has to give the rook back as 44...♖d2 45.b7 ♘g4? is parried by 46.♗f4+.

5. Arizmendi-Raetsky
Llucmajor 2019

39.♖dh3 ♖d3 leads to equality, but **39.♖c1!** overloads the black queen: **39...♕xc1 40.♕e6+ ♔f8** Black pinned his last hopes on 41.♖f3+ ♕f4, but **41.♖h3!** forced him to resign.

6. Michalik-Velicka
Prague (rapid) 2019

31.♖xh7! ♘xe5 32.♕h6! And White won. More challenging was 31...♔xh7 (31...♖xf3 32.♕h6!) 32.♕f7+ ♔h8 33.♖e1! (33.♖xe6 ♖xf3! 34.♔xf3 ♕c3+ 35.♔e3 ♕c6) 33...♖c1 34.♖xe6 or 34.♗d1, winning.

7. Dreev-Loiacono
Forni di Sopra 2019

10.e4! ♕xd4 10...♕e6 11.♗c4 or 10...♕d6 11.♕b3. **11.♕b3! ♘xe4** The critical test – 11...♕xe5 12.♕xb7 is completely hopeless as well. **12.♕xf7+ ♔d8 13.♖a5+** Black resigned in view of 13...b6 14.♖d1.

8. Rodshtein-Amin
France 2019

35.f6! gxf6 36.♗f5! 36.♖cc7 ♖c8 or 36.♖xh7+ ♔g8 37.♗f5 ♖c8! would give Black chances to survive. Now he is helpless against the 7th rank invasion. **36...♘d5 37.♖xh7+ ♔g8 38.♖d7! ♔h8 39.♗e6 e4 40.♖xd5 e3 41.♖xd2** Black resigned.

9. Kunin-Sonis
Radenci 2019

57.♗f6! ♗xg7 To 57...♗d6 White replies 58.♕g5! ♖xe5+ 59.♗xe5 ♕b6 60.♗h7+! ♔xh7 61.♕h5+, mating. **58.♕g5 ♔f8 59.♕xg7+ ♔e8 60.♗c6+!** And Black resigned in view of 60...♕xc6 61.♕g8+ ♔d7 62.♕xd8 mate.

ARTHUR VAN DE OUDEWEETERING

I double-dare you!

Inflicting doubled pawns on yourself by offering a queen exchange: why would you do that?

Our attachment to sound pawn structures often keep us from even considering, let alone playing, a move that would damage our own structure. But counter-intuitive decisions can make sense, as the following fragment, from a Mark Dvoretsky exercise, convincingly shows.

Adorjan-Lukacs
Hungary 1970
position after 23...♔g7

24.♕d3! ♕d5 After 24...♕xd3 25.cxd3 ♖f7 26.♖e6 c5 27.♔f1 ♖d7 28.♔e2 White's pawn structure is of less importance than the obvious difference in activity of the rooks. Besides, Black should definitely worry about the pawn ending after 24...♕xd3 25.♖e7+ ♔f7 26.♖xf7+ ♔xf7 27.cxd3 when White seems to have a dangerous majority on the kingside despite the doubled f-pawns. **25.♕xd5!** A second surprise. White improves his opponent's pawn structure. **25...cxd5 26.♖e6 ♖f7 27.♔f1** It becomes clear that White's activity is constricting Black even more than after 24...♕xd3. White proceeded to score a smooth win.

27...h5 28.h3 hxg4 29.hxg4 a5 30.a4 ♖d7 31.♔e2 ♔f7 32.♔d3 ♖d8 33.♖c6 ♖d7 34.♔d4 ♔g7 35.f3 ♔f7 36.c3 ♔e7 37.b4 axb4 38.cxb4 ♔f7 39.a5 bxa5 40.bxa5 ♖e7 41.a6 1-0.
Truly impressive play from the 20-year-old Adorjan.

Keep this general idea in mind, while we go to the middlegame and step things up a bit, allowing even isolated doubled pawns. Here's one from another well-known 20-year-old.

Botvinnik-Sorokin
Moscow 1931
position after 19...e5

20.♕e3! As Botvinnik himself wrote: 'In the 7 years that I had been playing chess, this is probably the most subtle positional move I managed to make'. True, but White had other moves that are even stronger. Sergey Smokti has suggested 20.♖d6. The quiet 20.h3 (Kosikov), and certainly the more simple and straightforward 20.♖c2 (Voronkov), pushing back Black's pieces after, for example, 20...♕e7 21.♕e3, are other strong alternatives. **20...♕xe3 21.fxe3** As Botvinnik noted, Black can hardly contest the d-file now, while the pawns on e5 and f7 are easier to target. But Black could have put up tougher resistance later on: **21...♗g4 22.a5 ♘c8 23.♖c1 ♗xf3?!** Better was 23...♖e8. **24.gxf3 ♘e7 25.♘d5**

25...♘c6? Voluntarily making a lot of strategic concessions. Now White has free play. Meanwhile, 25...♘fxd5 would have yielded Black good fighting chances: 26.exd5 ♖fc8 (26...♘f5 27.d6 ♘xe3 28.♖c7) or 26.♗xd5 ♘xd5 27.exd5 ♖ac8 28.♖dc2 ♖cd8!?. **26.♘xf6+ gxf6 27.♖d7 ♖ab8 28.♔f2**

Now clearly White's strategy has succeeded, and Botvinnik skilfully converted his advantage (1-0, 55).

Don't let isolated doubled pawns automatically keep you from offering an exchange of queens.

Perhaps nowadays we are more used to doubled e-pawns, one dynamic advantage being the control of central squares. For instance, Botvinnik's e3-pawn deprived Black's c6-knight of the d4-square. Anyway, Botvinnik's original idea to voluntarily create a static weakness was impressive enough to find its way into many manuals.

Here's a different example, where you have to look harder for the dynamics compensating the doubled pawn.

Mednis-Bouaziz
Riga 1979
position after 16...♕c4

17.♕d3! ♕xd3 18.cxd3 It would seem that Mednis copied the idea from Smyslov, who used it in a slightly different position to inflict an almost traditional first-round loss on Tal in the historic Candidates Tournament of 1959. But no! In the Russian tournament book, Mednis refers to Geller-Martinovic, Nis 1977, which had seen 16...♕b5 17.♕d3 ♕b4, a game now not even in the databases, but from a tournament in which Mednis participated as well. Those were the days! **18...g6 19.♖c3** As in the Smyslov game, it appears that Black cannot contend the just opened c-file and will soon be forced to improve White's damaged pawn structure. **19...♖xc3 20.bxc3 ♖c8**

21.♖c1!? Now the exact same position as in 1959 has been reached, when Tal met Smyslov's 21.c4 with 21...e4!? 22.dxe4 ♖xc4 and White was still pressing after 23.♘d2. **21...♘e8 22.g4 ♘c5? 23.♘xc5 dxc5 24.c4** Now White's spatial advantage and half-open b-file yield a clear advantage, which Mednis duly converted (1-0, 64).

In *In Search of Harmony* Smyslov modestly called his 15.♕d3 'the correct treatment of the position'. I'm more inclined to go with Ragozin and Gligoric: 'A deep assessment of the situation!'

Similarly, a half-open b-file may give sufficient impetus to accept even isolated doubled rook pawns. Here you would have to be pretty confident about your dynamic chances, because no doubled pawns can become more static than those on the edge of the board.

Eljanov-Carlsen
Wijk aan Zee 2017
position after 12...♕e7

13.♕a3! A novelty in this exact position, but we can be sure that it hardly came as a surprise to Magnus. After all, 13.♘e5 ♘bd7 14.♕a3 had been played here before, while in Tilburg 1990, Andersson ground down Short in an endgame arising from a Stonewall after the same queen exchange. **13...♕xa3 14.bxa3** It is a bonus for White, of course, that he will no longer have to fear a kingside attack, which is also one of the standard goals that a queen exchange aims for in general. **14...♘bd7 15.♖ab1** Again White has a very pleasant endgame due to the pressure along the half-open b-file and his spatial advantage. Eljanov got a large advantage, and even managed to exchange his forward doubled a-pawn in the follow-up: **15...♖b8 16.a4 a5 17.♖b2 ♘e4 18.♘xe4 dxe4 19.♘g5 ♖f6 20.f3 h6 21.♘h3 exf3 22.♗xf3 ♖f7 23.♘f2 c5 24.♘d3 cxd4 25.exd4 ♘f6 26.♘c5** 26.♘e5, followed by c4-c5, seems even stronger. **26...♘e4 27.♘xe6 ♗xa4**

Later on, Eljanov lost the thread and even spoilt the draw (0-1, 60), but that in no way detracts from his fine 13.♕a3!.

Conclusion
So, easier said than done, but don't let isolated doubled pawns automatically keep you from offering an exchange of queens. It may pay off to dive deeply into a position to detect the possible ensuing dynamics as shown in the above examples. ∎

**A world-class gathering
at a private party**

The spirit of Amber in Amsterdam

Ilya and Adele Levitov with their young son and their special guests in front of the Waldorf Astoria: Anish Giri, Evgeny Bareev, Boris Gelfand, Vladimir Kramnik, Vishy Anand, Peter Svidler, Alexander Grischuk and Ian Nepomniachtchi.

The Levitov Chess Week will in all likelihood go down in history as the most unusual chess tournament of 2019. Eight top GMs competed at the Waldorf Astoria in Amsterdam, almost unnoticed, including Vladimir Kramnik, who briefly came out of retirement. **DIRK JAN TEN GEUZENDAM** joined the happy few.

What do you do to celebrate your 40th birthday? For Ilya Levitov it was an apt moment to make an old dream reality: to organize a private chess tournament. A tournament just for himself, a fine selection of grandmasters that he knew well, family and friends, and invited guests. In grand surroundings with nothing left to desire. His inspiration was the exclusive Amber tournament in Monaco that he had visited several times and where the players worked in secluded luxury and enjoyed each other's company after the games.

But he even went a step further. There was no need for spectators and the games were not broadcast live. In the evening, the games were sent to the main chess platforms and a daily recap by Peter Svidler was posted on YouTube (quite incredible, as Svidler also played himself and arrived jet-lagged in Amsterdam on the morning of the first day). In the meantime, everything was recorded by an omnipresent camera crew for a film by a leading Russian documentary maker.

Hanging out with the guys

Levitov had no wish to keep the event a secret; he just wanted his grandmaster friends to feel at ease and be allowed to create games that would not be rated. As he explained: 'For some reason I am upset with the situation in the chess world, especially with the role of the grandmasters. It's nobody's fault. The development of computer programs has made it clear that the grandmasters are no longer the magicians of the past, who knew more than the people who are watching the games. Now they know less. It's not that I don't want anybody to watch it, I just wanted to create a cosier atmosphere, so that they would feel as if they were playing more or less at home.'

And there was an added motivation: 'Lately I have been feeling that chess is not a sport. It's more like an art, a social occasion; it's a game. And there is a big difference between sport and a game. Football is a game, but it's mostly sport. You're for somebody, you love some team, you want them to win. I don't see chess this way. It's more of a social thing, an intellectual thing. All this competitiveness at the top level, which has always been there – who is first in the rankings – I am not particularly interested in this aspect. For me it's much more important to hang out with the guys, because they are very interesting

'Chess is not for everybody. The game itself resists becoming too popular.'

people. I like being around chess players. That's my motivation for the tournament.'

Ilya Levitov's passion for chess first came to the attention of a wider circle when, together with Evgeny Bareev, he wrote the award-winning modern classic *From London to Elista* (2007), a gripping insider account of the World Championship matches that Vladimir Kramnik won against Kasparov, Leko and Topalov. And from 2010 to 2014 he was the Executive Director of the Russian Chess Federation. In this capacity, he organized top-level events like the Tal Memorial and the 2012 World Championship match between Anand and Gelfand.

This time, his wish to organize a gathering of top players was purely private and had nothing to do with an urge to promote chess. 'Honestly speaking, I do not believe in the promotion of chess, because it's a very complex game. Chess, like classical music, is not for everybody. And there's nothing wrong with that. It's the best you can say about anything in the world right now, because everything is for everybody now. Chess is not for everybody. The game itself resists becoming too popular.'

Post-mortems returned!

The 'Levitov Chess Week' comprised three days of rapid chess, preceded by a blitz tournament and a classical

Chess for fun in the hospitality room with Genna Sosonko, Jeroen Piket, Peter and Olga Svidler, Jan Gustafsson, Judit Polgar and Anish Giri.

NEW IN CHESS

music concert by world-renowned musicians flown in from Moscow. For his venue, Levitov had chosen the Amsterdam Waldorf Astoria, an oasis of rest and luxury spread over six connected historical houses on Herengracht, the street along the city's most prestigious canal. Each round was divided into two two-game sessions, and at the request of the host, the players not playing followed the action in the hospitality room.

This, as Svidler noted, had a remarkable effect: post-mortems returned! Said Svidler: 'If you stop to think about it, it's really not a miracle that they disappeared. You just feel the futility of it, because you know you can spend two hours shuffling around pieces and then the computer will give you the answer in a couple of seconds. But when they do come back, it's very enjoyable, because this is a company of people who have known each other for ages, and for us to just sit at the board and discuss chess is very enjoyable. '

Not only chess-technical issues were discussed; there was also a lot of reminiscing, which actually added some useful footnotes to chess history. One day, the story was told of a young Kramnik who had gone out late during the 1993 VSB tournament in Amsterdam. He had done so in the company of Ivan Sokolov and it had been so late that Sokolov had spent the night in Kramnik's room. When Kramnik woke up, he asked who he was playing and with barely concealed worry, Sokolov said, 'Anand, with Black'. To which Kramnik replied, 'Ah, Anand with Black, couldn't be better!' A nice story, but Levitov added an important detail. It had not been a show of youthful self-confidence, but a sign of relief, since Kramnik had already prepared his opening for Anand.

And on the subject of Kramnik preparation, Anand revealed why 'Vladi' had made a very short draw

Vishy Anand and Peter Svidler in a light-hearted mood at the start of their last-round game that would end in an atypical loss in 23 moves for the former World Champion.

with the white pieces in his 1994 Candidates match against Yudasin, after he had won the first game with Black. Before the game, his second Tseshkovsky had provided him with a useful suggestion in the Sveshnikov, but in the playing hall Kramnik discovered – as he should have known, of course – that he was playing White!

Back to his best years

Only the youngsters Giri and Nepomniachtchi found it hard to completely detach themselves from their beloved

'For us to just sit at the board and discuss chess is very enjoyable.'

laptops. The Dutchman even had it with him all the time. Perhaps not surprisingly, the fight for first place in

the final round was between them and Alexander Grischuk who, besides the starting fees, had persuaded Levitov to have a prize-fund and proved once more that such a stimulus works for him. 'Nepo' and Grischuk finished with the same number of points, but Nepomniachtchi was declared the winner of the 5,000 euro first prize on tiebreak.

At the end of this article, Nepomniachtchi annotates his win against Kramnik and has an interesting suggestion for Ilya Levitov in case he is going to organize another event. But first we'll look at some further highlights from a memorable tournament that produced a fine harvest of creative games. The notes are based on Peter Svidler's daily YouTube recaps and suggestions by Anish Giri.

To begin with, a win by Anand against his old rival, about which Svidler said: 'It felt like Vishy was back to his best years.' After the second day Anand was half a point behind the leading Nepomniachtchi, but the Indian dropped back on the final day.

Vishy Anand
Vladimir Kramnik
Amsterdam rapid 2019 (4)
Italian Game, Giuoco Piano

**1.e4 e5 2.♘f3 ♘c6 3.♗c4 ♗c5
4.0-0 ♘f6 5.d3 d6 6.c3 a6 7.a4
♗a7 8.♖e1 0-0 9.h3 h6 10.♘bd2
♗e6 11.♗xe6 fxe6 12.b4 ♘h5
13.♖a2 ♘f4 14.♘c4 b5 15.♗xf4**

15...bxc4?
Better was 15...♖xf4, but Kramnik
probably felt that after 16.♘cd2
White's play on the queenside
was more promising than Black's
counter-chances on the kingside.
**16.♗e3 ♗xe3 17.♖xe3 cxd3
18.♕xd3**

But this is a very pleasant position for
White, and with pointed play Anand
further increases his influence on
the queenside. Watch how his knight
on f3 will soon occupy a dominant
position on c6!
**18...♘e7 19.c4! ♕b8 20.♕d2
♕b7 21.♘e1 ♖ad8 22.b5 ♘g6**
After 22...c6, 23.♖b2 cements White's
advantage.
**23.♘d3 axb5 24.cxb5 ♖a8
25.♘b4**

25...♘f4
25...♘e7 was a better defence, but also
insufficient after 26.♘a6!, when c7
and d6 are too vulnerable.
26.♘c6

There it is, exerting very annoying
pressure and making the passed
a-pawn an even bigger force. In fact,
it will be unstoppable.
**26...♘h7 27.♔h2 ♖f6 28.g3 ♘g6
29.♖b3 ♘f8 30.a5 ♘d7 31.a6
♕c8 32.♕e2 ♕e8 33.♖f3**

Trading off pieces only makes the
situation on the queenside worse for
Black.
**33...♕f7 34.♖xf6 gxf6 35.♖c2
♘b6 36.♘a5 f5 37.♖c6 ♖f8
38.♕c2** Now there is only one way
left to cling on to the c-pawn.

38...♘a8 39.exf5 exf5
But now Anand sacrifices one of his
queenside pawns to fatally undermine Black's position.

**40.b6! cxb6 41.♘c4 ♔g7
42.♖xd6 f4 43.g4 f3 44.♕e4**

Now Black's only move is 44...♕f4+,
but after the exchange of queens his
position is in ruins, so he resigned.

Don't tease Kramnik
Vladimir Kramnik was inevitably a
bit rusty, but was ready to strike when
the opportunity arose. Before this
game, his friends were teasing him
with his play on the first day, which
may have had some effect.

Peter Svidler
Vladimir Kramnik
Amsterdam rapid 2019 (6)
Queen's Indian Defence

**1.c4 e6 2.♘f3 ♘f6 3.b3 b6 4.♗b2
♗b7 5.e3 ♗e7 6.d4 0-0 7.♗d3
c5 8.0-0 cxd4 9.exd4 d5 10.♘c3
dxc4 11.bxc4 ♘c6 12.♖c1**
One of several choices White has
here. Svidler also mentioned 12.♕e2.
12...♖c8

13.♕e2? This move leads to trouble. White should have played 13.♖e1!, with the idea to meet 13...♘b4 with 14.♗f1, when after 14...♗xf3 15.♕xf3 ♕xd4 White has the strong 16.♘d5.
13...♘b4! A knight sortie that is quite unpleasant for White.

After the game Kramnik surprised Svidler by telling him that he had actually considered taking on d4. To make sure that no one will ever make this well-known mistake, Svidler showed the instructive punishment in his daily recap: 13...♘xd4? 14.♘xd4 ♕xd4 15.♘d5 ♕c5 16.♗xf6

ANALYSIS DIAGRAM

16...♗xf6 (also disastrous is 16... gxf6 17.♘xe7+ ♕xe7 18.♕g4+ ♔h8 19.♕h4, and the only way to stop 20.♕xh7 mate is 19...f5, which loses the queen) 17.♕e4. Again lethally eyeing h7: 17...g6 18.♘xf6+ ♔g7 19.♕xb7, and Black is a piece down.
14.♗b1 ♗xf3 15.gxf3
Because 15.♕xf3 ♖xc4 is not really an option. White seems to be holding some trump cards: the bishop pair and possible attacking chances along the g-file, too. But Kramnik finds a very strong continuation:
15...♘h5! 16.a3?

Vladimir Kramnik briefly came out of retirement to meet old friends and, despite being a bit rusty, showing sparks of great chess.

Hoping for 16...♘c6 17.d5, and things don't look all that bad for White. But Black does not need to withdraw the knight.

White should have tried 16.♘e4, when Kramnik was planning to play 16...♗g5 17.♖c3 ♘f4, and although White is still in the game, this is a very unpleasant position to play.

16...♗d6! A killer. Suddenly White is totally lost. What to do against the threat of ...♕g5+, followed by ...♕f4, is the first question.
17.f4 Because 17.♘e4 ♕h4 18.♘xd6 ♘f4 was hopeless.

Another try that won't work was 17.♕e4 f5 18.♕xe6+ ♔h8, and all the threats are there again. Svidler gave the following nice line: 19.♘e2 ♖c6 (threatening 20...♗xf2+) 20.♕e3 ♗xh2+ 21.♔xh2 ♕h4+, followed by ...♖g6+, and wins.

17...♕h4! An aesthetic way to win.
18.f3 After 18.axb4 ♘xf4 19.♕f3 ♘e2+ it's mate on h2.
18...♘xf4 19.♕d2

19...♘bd3 A nice final shot. 0-1.

Rolling down the queenside

At 52, Evgeny Bareev was the oldest participant. After the following flashy win he thanked his daughters and grandchild, who had come to

Amsterdam with him. This was the first game of his they watched in the hospitality room, and he urged them to do so more often.

Evgeny Bareev
Boris Gelfand
Amsterdam rapid 2019 (6)
Queen's Indian Defence
1.d4 ♘f6 2.c4 e6 3.♘f3 b6 4.♘c3 ♗b7 5.♗f4 ♗e7 6.e3 ♘h5 7.♗g3 d6 8.d5!?

8...e5?! An understandable reply, but 8...♗f6! was stronger.
9.♘d2 g6 10.♗e2 ♘xg3 11.hxg3 ♘d7 12.g4! Forceful play, killing Black's kingside pawn mobility.
12...♗f6 13.♕c2 ♗g7 14.0-0-0 a6 15.♖h3 ♕e7 16.♔b1 0-0-0
With the open h-file, it's understandable that Black castles queenside. But how safe is the king there?

17.e4! Now Black has no breaks and White will come rolling down the queenside. **17...♔b8 18.b4** Here we come. **18...♘f6 19.♘b3 ♗c8 20.♖g3 h5 21.g5 ♘d7** The white g-pawn may get lost at some point, but that's not what Bareev was worrying about.

22.c5!? Making no secret of his intentions. More cautious would have been 22.♘a4, followed by ♖c3, to prepare the advance of the c-pawn.
22...dxc5 23.d6! cxd6 24.♘d5 ♕e6 25.b5!

25...♗b7 Hoping to weather the storm by giving a pawn, when the white a-pawn might actually protect the black king. 25...a5 was clearly no option in view of 26.♘xa5!, followed by ♕a4 and ♕xa5, plus mate. Almost all white pieces are ready to join the attack, whereas Black's are mostly offside.
26.bxa6 ♗xd5

27.♖xd5 As pointed out by Svidler, more direct would have been 27.a7+ ♔xa7 28.♖xd5, and once the knight frees the way for the rook to the a-file, Black will be unable to save himself.
27...♔a7 28.♗c4 ♕e7 29.a4 Another invader joins the fray.

Evgeny Bareev with his daughters Anya and Olya and grandson Vova (Anya's son), who inspired him to create a classy attacking game against Boris Gelfand.

29...♘b8 A better defensive attempt was 29...♘f8!?, although White retains good attacking chances after, for instance, 30.♘c1 ♘e6 31.♘e2 ♘d4 32.♕b2 h4 33.♖b3!?.

30.♗b5!
Now White will soon crash through.

30...h4 31.♖gd3 ♕xg5 There goes the pawn; but the real action is on the other side of the board.

32.a5 ♗f8 33.axb6+ ♚xb6
Time to wrap up:

34.♘xc5 ♚a7 35.♘b7 ♕e7 36.♘xd8 ♕xd8 37.♕c5+ ♕b6 38.♕xb6+ ♚xb6 39.♖b3 ♚a7 40.♗c4 And Black resigned.

Fighting Nepo

In the last round but one, Giri had to beat Nepomniachtchi to catch up with him and Grischuk. He did so, but in the final round 'Nepo' decided the fight for first in his favour anyway.

Anish Giri
Ian Nepomniachtchi
Amsterdam rapid 2019 (6)
Caro-Kann Defence

1.e4 c6 A regular choice of Nepomniachtchi of late.

2.♘f3 d5 3.d3

Spectating was an exclusive activity at the Waldorf Astoria, but besides Svidler's YouTube recaps an ever-present camera crew collected tons of footage for a chess film.

A rather unusual continuation, offering a queen swap and hoping for an edge in the resulting middlegame.

3...dxe4 4.dxe4 ♕xd1+ 5.♚xd1 ♘f6 6.♘fd2 ♘g4 7.♚e1! e5 8.♘c4

8...b5 8...♗c5? looks tempting, but fails to 9.f3! ♘f2 10.b4! ♗d4 11.c3, and once Black has taken on h1 and White has taken the bishop, the black

knight, together with Black, will be lost.

9.♘e3 ♗c5 10.♘xg4 ♗xg4 11.a4!

White has a very pleasant position thanks to the weak black queenside pawns and squares.

11...b4 12.a5!? ♘d7 13.♗c4 ♚e7 14.♘d2

14...♗d6? This loses two tempi.

After 14...♗d4 15.f3 ♗e6 16.♗xe6 ♔xe6 White would still be better, but Black's situation would be less problematic than in the game.

15.f3 ♗e6 16.♗xe6 ♔xe6 17.♘c4 ♖ab8 18.♔e2 ♗c5 19.♖d1 f6 20.♗e3 ♗xe3 21.♔xe3

The situation doesn't look dramatic yet for Black, but White's advantage is considerable, thanks to his more active pieces.

21...♔e7 22.♖d6 ♖hc8 23.♖ad1 ♘c5 24.g3! Opening a second front.

24...♖c7? Black could have put up more resistance with 24...♖d8! 25.f4 ♘b7. **25.f4 exf4+ 26.gxf4 ♖b5?** **27.♖g1 g6 28.f5** Now Black's kingside is ripped open. **28...b3 29.c3 ♔f7**

30.e5! The winning breakthrough. The rest was not too complicated.

30...fxe5 31.fxg6+ ♔g7 32.gxh7+ ♔xh7 33.♖dg6 ♖b8 34.♖6g5 ♔h8 35.♖xe5 ♘a4 36.♖a1 ♘xc3 37.bxc3 ♖h7 38.♔d4 ♖xh2 39.♖b1 ♖h3 40.♘d6 ♖d8 41.♖e8+ Black resigned.

NOTES BY
Ian Nepomniachtchi

Vladimir Kramnik
Ian Nepomniachtchi
Amsterdam rapid 2019 (3)
Queen's Pawn Opening

1.♘f3

One of my favourite events was the Amber Tournament, where leading grandmasters competed not only at rapid chess, but also at blindfold play. Such an unusual format was very much to my liking, and I always read the reports from there with great interest. Alas, I never managed to play there, but thanks to the Levitov Chess

I would like to take the opportunity to suggest that blindfold chess is added next year.

Week I was able partially to experience the atmosphere of the chess festival, which, as Ilya himself said, he wanted to recreate in Amsterdam. I would like to hope that the tournament will become a traditional one, and to thank Ilya for an excellent beginning! And I would like to take the opportunity to suggest that blindfold chess is added as one of the disciplines next year.

1...d5 2.d4 ♗f5

An interesting set-up, in which it is not so easy for White to pose problems for his opponent – especially in games with a shortened time control. **3.c4 e6 4.♘c3 ♘c6!?** This move is advocated by grandmasters Indjic and Li Chao. Previously I had exclusively played 4...♘f6. But the most popular continuation is 4...c6, as, for example, Morozevich has played.

5.cxd5!?

In principle, Black is not averse to capturing on d5 with a piece, so it may be interesting to deny him this additional possibility.

5...exd5 6.♗f4 ♗d6 7.♗g3!?

7.♘xd5 ♗e4 8.♘c3 ♗xf3 9.♗xd6 ♕xd6 10.gxf3 ♕xd4, and White can hope for a minimal advantage, Aronian-Li Chao, Moscow 2016.

7...♘f6 In my view, 7...♘ce7 8.e3 c6 is a more accurate move order: then Black is not threatened with any pins on the h4-d8 diagonal.

8.e3 ♘e7 9.♗h4 ♘e4

9...c6 10.♗xf6 gxf6 leads to a well-known structure from the Queen's Gambit, where the limit of Black's dreams is a draw somewhere around the hundred move mark.

10.♗d3

A restrained move. Important variations arise after 10.♘xd5 ♘xd5 and now:

ANALYSIS DIAGRAM

A) 11.♗xd8 ♗b4+ 12.♔e2 ♘dc3+ 13.bxc3 ♘xc3+ 14.♔e1 (14.♔d2? is bad because of 14...♘xa2+ 15.♔e2 ♘c3+) 14...♘xd1+ 15.♔xd1 ♖xd8, and the advantage of the two bishops allows Black thoughts about not just equalizing;

B) 11.♗b5+ ♗d7 12.♗xd8 ♗b4+ 13.♔f1 ♗xb5+ 14.♔g1 ♘ec3 15.bxc3 ♘xc3 16.♕c2 ♘e2+ 17.♕xe2 ♗xe2 18.♗xc7 ♖c8 19.♗g3 b5 with an unclear position.

10...c6?!
This allows the opponent to create unpleasant tension in the centre. After 10...♘xc3 11.bxc3 ♗xd3 12.♕xd3 0-0 13.♖b1 b6 White retains some pressure.

11.♕c2

11...♕a5?
Virtually the only move leading to a decent position is 11...♗b4 12.0-0 ♘d6 13.♗xf5 ♘xf5 14.♗xe7 ♘xe7 15.♕b3 ♗xc3 16.bxc3 ♕c7.

12.♗xe7 ♗xe7
A choice of two evils: 12...♔xe7 13.0-0

♘xc3 14.♗xf5 ♘b5 15.e4, with an enormous advantage for White.

13.0-0 ♘xc3 14.♗xf5 ♘b5 15.♘e5 ♕c7
15...g6 fails to 16.♘xc6 ♕c7 17.♘xe7.

16.♗xh7 ♗f6 17.f4 0-0-0

Vladimir and I hardly harboured any doubts about the result of the game. I realized that I had to rejoice over a small achievement: I had nevertheless managed to castle!

18.♗d3 ♘d6 19.♖ac1 ♔b8 20.b4 ♕e7 21.a4 ♖c8
Somewhere around here I finally realized that the game would not end immediately. Yes, Black is a pawn down, at the same time he has a bad

position... but nevertheless in rapid chess even a small spark of counterplay can kindle a big fire.

22.♕b3?
White falls into what is probably the only trap. The solid move 22.♕f2 deprives Black of even illusory chances of displaying activity.

22...♗xe5 23.dxe5 f6
It stands to reason that Black cannot solve all his problems, but to force the opponent to defend a little is an unprecedented success by the standards of the course of this game.

24.♕c3
24.exd6?? is not possible because of 24...♕xe3+ 25.♔h1 ♖xh2+.

When in Amsterdam... Ilya and Adele Levitov decided that a boat was the perfect place to hand Ian Nepomniachtchi the winner's trophy and have the closing dinner.

24...♘f7 25.♗f5 ♖c7 26.exf6 gxf6

27.♕f3 After avoiding an unpleasant thrust, Vladimir began making solid (and strong!) moves.
27...♘d6 28.♗d3 ♖d8
The rook on the third rank excellently defends the kingside against any encroachments, but it is somewhat cut off from the centre of the board, to where Black switches the theatre of operations.
29.♕d4 ♘e4 30.♖h3

30...a5! Sink or swim!
31.bxa5 c5 32.♕b2 c4
Objectively the advantage is still with White, but the scene has changed. He has not managed to avert the oppo-

nent's desperate breakthrough, and for a human the position has become extremely unclear.
33.♗xe4 33.♗c2 ♖g8! with compensation for Black.
33...dxe4

34.♖h5? I thought that this move was the most logical, since the rook must be brought into play as quickly as possible, but, strangely enough, now White loses.
34.♖g3! would have retained an advantage. It looks awkward, but the intention is revealed in the variation 34...c3 35.♖xc3 ♖d1+ 36.♔f2 ♕d8, and now 37.♖g8! ♕xg8 38.♖xc7 ♕d5 (38...♔xc7 39.♕c2+) 39.♕c2 and wins. But with the rook on h5 a similar idea does not work. Of course, Black is not obliged to play 34...c3, but then White acquires time to safeguard his king and set up a blockade of the c-pawn. However, Black's position remains quite playable.
34...c3!
Now, after using nearly all of his remaining time, Kramnik played:
35.♖xc3 but there is no longer any way of saving the game.
35...♖d1+ 36.♔f2 ♕d8

37.♔g3 37.♖h8? ♕xh8 38.♖xc7 ♕h4+ and mate next move.
The best chance was the desperate 37.♔e2, when to win Black would have had to find 37...♖g7! 38.g3 (the escape square for the king is blocked) 38...♖gd7 39.♖c2 ♖h7!.

ANALYSIS DIAGRAM

I am not sure that I would have coped ☺.
37...♖d2 38.♕b3 Black also wins after 38.♕xd2 ♖g7+ 39.♔h4 ♕xd2 40.♖h8+ ♔a7 41.♖cc8 b5 42.♖a8+ ♔b7 43.♖ab8+ ♔c7 44.♖bc8+ ♔d6 45.♖hd8+ ♖d7 46.axb5 ♕f2+ 47.♔h3 ♕xe3+.
38...♖g7+ 39.♔h3 ♖gxg2 40.♕f7 f5

The king has nowhere to hide from the quick mate. White resigned. ∎

Amsterdam rapid 2019				1	2	3	4	5	6	7	8		cat. XXI
													TPR
1 Ian Nepomniachtchi	IGM	RUS	2773	*	1	0	1	½	1	½	1	5	2886
2 Alexander Grischuk	IGM	RUS	2788	0	*	½	1	½	1	1	1	5	2884
3 Anish Giri	IGM	NED	2730	1	½	*	½	½	½	½	1	4½	2837
4 Vishy Anand	IGM	IND	2757	0	0	½	*	1	1	0	1	3½	2734
5 Boris Gelfand	IGM	ISR	2702	½	½	½	0	*	1	1	0	3½	2742
6 Vladimir Kramnik	IGM	RUS	2756	0	0	½	0	0	*	1	1	2½	2635
7 Peter Svidler	IGM	RUS	2727	½	0	½	1	0	0	*	½	2½	2640
8 Evgeny Bareev	IGM	CAN	2664	0	0	0	0	1	0	½	*	1½	2532

The Blitz Whisperer
Maxim Dlugy

Learning from the Best

Games are often more instructive if the players differ considerably in strength and the mistakes can easily be pointed out. The same goes for blitz, argues **MAXIM DLUGY** as he tells us what he learnt from the Paris leg of the Grand Chess Tour.

A s I started looking over the blitz games from the Paris leg of the Grand Chess Tour, I realized that these amazing players are all capable of providing us with excellent instruction, even by showcasing their own blitz games. In fact, I maintain that it's possible to learn much more from blitz games than most chess authors would imagine. The reason is that it's always far easier to understand the concept of a certain mistake if the punishment for it is shown in very destructive fashion.

This is also why, for example, I found Mikhail Botvinnik's collection of best games so instructive. His opponents were generally 200 to 300 points lower-rated than him, and this provided excellent instructional value.

The same applies to blitz, where the resistance level is much weaker, as you don't have much time. And the blitz in Paris was no different.

We start with a fascinating struggle from the last round between Fabiano Caruana and Alexander Grischuk.

Fabiano Caruana
Alexander Grischuk
Paris 2019 (18)
Caro-Kann Defence, Advance Variation

1.e4 c6 2.d4 d5 3.e5 ♗f5 4.♘c3 e6 5.g4 ♗g6 6.♘ge2

Caruana chooses one of the most aggressive lines in the Advanced Variation of the Caro-Kann, popularized by John Nunn and Alexei Shirov. Grischuk will have to dig deep to remember all the key defensive ideas here.

6...c5 7.h4 h5 8.♘f4 ♗h7 9.♘xh5 ♘c6 10.dxc5 ♗xc5 11.♗g5

This move, a novelty at GM level, really starts the game, because Grischuk himself played 11.♗g2 against Bareev some time back.

11...♕c7

The move played in the one game in the database, 11...♕b6, could lead to a very complicated position for Black after 12.♘xg7+ ♔f8 13.♘xe6+ fxe6 14.♕f3+ ♔e8 15.0-0-0.

12.f4

Another way to play the position is to complete development with 12.♗d3 ♕xe5+ 13.♔f1 ♗xd3+ 14.♕xd3, when Black's extra pawn is offset by White's better king position and development.

12...d4?

Fabi's prep pays off, as Sasha loses his way. It was important to fight for the g1-a7 diagonal with 12...♕b6. As 13.♗d3 would allow a nice resource: 13...♗g1!, forcing White to go for a repetition with 14.♘e2 ♕f2+, followed by 15...♕e3+, White's best fighting chance would seem to be 13.♗e2 ♕xb2 14.♘a4 ♗b4+ 15.♔f2 ♕xc2 16.♘xg7+ ♔f8 17.♘h5 ♕xd1 18.♗xd1, with a very complicated position, as White's domination on the kingside fully compensates for the sacrificed pawn.

13.♘b5 ♕a5+ 14.♕d2 ♘b4

15.♘a3??

As it turns out, the position was already winning for White, as Black's pieces have got themselves completely penned in. The correct move here was 15.♖c1!, simply threatening to play 16.♘d6+, after which the ♘xg7+ threat, coupled with the transition to an endgame with a3, would be too much for Black.

15...♗xc2? Grischuk misses an important tactic! After 15...♘d3+! 16.♗xd3 ♗b4 White must lose or sacrifice his queen, but the best compensation he will get will only preserve the balance. After 17.♗b5+ ♔f8 18.f5! exf5 19.0-0-0 ♗xd2+ 20.♗xd2 ♕b6 21.e6! ♘e7 22.exf7 ♗g6 23.♖de1 ♗xf7 24.♗b4 ♖e8! the position is wildly unclear, and White's best moves would be harder to find.

16.♘c4?!

It seems that evacuating the king is White's top priority. After 16.♗b5+ ♔f8 17.0-0 Black should probably shed an exchange with 17...♖xh5 18.gxh5 ♗f5, with good compen-

From the way he resigned you could see how thoroughly Alexander Grischuk enjoyed his last blitz game in Paris against Fabiano Caruana, even though he lost.

sation for the material, although if White manages to double rooks on the g-file, Black's position may not feel so rosy after all.

16...♕a4 17.♔f2

Fabi has decided that the safest square for the king is g3, whereupon he can start developing the rest of his pieces.

17...d3+?

It's hard to spot, but Black can simply go after White's knight on h5 if he keeps the d4-pawn where it is. After the defensive 17...♔f8 18.♔g3 ♗g6!, planning to take on h5, Black seems to have a good game.

18.♔g3 ♖xh5 19.gxh5 ♘e7 20.♗xe7 ♗xe7 21.♔g2 0-0-0

22.♘e3?!

The knight stood very well on c4 – overlooking the d6-square. It was strong to continue moving the king into safety with 22.♔h2, while planning to stabilize the knight with b3.

22...♔b8 23.♖hc1 ♗c5

23...f6 was also interesting to try and exploit White's king's position.

24.♖e1 ♕b5 25.♗e4 f5 26.exf6 gxf6 27.h6

I maintain that it's possible to learn much more from blitz games than most chess authors would imagine.

In positions where you cannot control the flow of ideas, try to create positive assets that can be relied on to deflect your opponent's attention. In this case, Fabiano shows that the h-pawn can become strong if Black does not attend to it.

27...f5 Black had many promising moves at his disposal, e.g. 27...♕e8 or 27...♗d6; but it's natural to sharpen it up when time is getting short.

28.♗f3 ♗d6 Objectively not the best, but in such a crazy position best moves are tough to come by.

29.♘g2?
Going back is often wrong. After 29.a3 e5 30.♘xf5 exf4+ 31.♔h2 ♕xf5 32.axb4 White is better, although not clear to the naked eye... unless you spot the plan of ♖g1-g7.

29...♕d7?! After 29...♕e8! 30.♔h2 ♕g6 Black is doing very well.

30.♔h3 Bringing the queen out with 30.♕c3 would have been very strong.

30...♘a6?!
Black should have hurried to knock off the h6-pawn. After 30...♖h8 31.a3 ♘d5 32.♗xd5 exd5 he would stand better.

31.♕e3 Once again bringing the queen out with 31.♕c3 was stronger. This reminds me of Jacob Aagaard's lecture at my academy recently: 1) Consider all your options, and 2) Bring out your pieces!

31...♘c7 32.♕d4! Finally Caruana moves his queen to the key diagonal.

32...♕h7 33.♖g7 ♕xg7 34.hxg7 ♖g8 35.♗d1?! The focus on the d-pawn is understandable, but extra exchanges are best converted by using open files. The strongest idea seems to be exactly that. After 35.♖g1! ♗c5 (to stop White's ♘e3, but now, unexpectedly, the h-pawn enters the fray) 36.h5 ♖xg7 37.♘e3 ♖xg1 38.♖xg1 ♗xe3 39.♖g8+ ♘e8 40.♖xe8+ ♔c7 41.h6 ♗xf4 42.♖xe6, White has an eventually winning endgame.

35...d2 36.♖e2 ♗e4 37.♖xd2 ♘d5 Black is down an exchange, but clearly has good chances to hold. With seconds left on both clocks, impulses take over.

DGT CENTAUR

The most innovative Chess Computer that automatically adapts itself to your playing strength.

Your Perfect Chess Friend!

With the sensor board you can simply move pieces in a natural way. Whether you are a beginner or an experienced player, whether you are a home player or a club player, Centaur always adapts to your level as soon as you make your first move!

✔ Fair chance to win
✔ Sensor board 40x40 cm
✔ e-Paper display
✔ Circular LED lights

Discover the DGT Centaur: digitalgametechnology.com

38.♗b3 ♖xg7 39.♗xd5 exd5 40.♖f1 ♗b4 41.♖e2 d4 42.♖ef2 ♗c5 43.a3 d3 44.♖d2 a5 45.♘e1 ♖d7 46.♘g2 a4 47.♖fd1 ♗b6

Black is completely fine after 47...♖g7 48.♘e1 ♗e3 49.♖g2 ♗xg2+ 50.♘xg2 ♗d4 51.♖xd3 ♗xb2.

48.♘e1 ♗a5 49.♖xd3

Finally Fabiano finds a way to sac an exchange to get some winning chances.

49...♗xd3 50.♖xd3

50...♖e7?

It was not obvious that Black's saving resource was to 'use all his pieces'. After 50...♔c7! 51.♖xd7+ ♔xd7 52.♘f3 ♗b6 53.h5 ♔e6 54.h6 ♗f6 55.h7 ♔g7 56.♘h4 ♔xh7 57.♘xf5 ♗c5 Black draws by simply trading all pawns on the queenside.

51.♘f3 ♖e2 52.h5 ♖xb2 53.♘e5 ♖b3 54.h6

It seems like the game is over, but suddenly Sasha finds an amazing resource.

54...♗c3 55.h7 The sly 55.♘h4 ♗xe5 56.♖d8+ ♔c7 57.fxe5 would have won quickly, but Fabi wasn't expecting anything special.

55...♗xe5 56.♖xb3 axb3 57.fxe5 b2 58.h8♕+ ♔a7!

Suddenly it becomes a game regardless, because White has to convert this better queen+pawn ending. Still, Fabi is up to the task.

59.e6 b1♕ 60.♕e5 ♕h1+ 61.♔g3 ♕g1+ 62.♔f3 ♕f1+

Of course, Black could have tried to get the queen to e7 after a series of checks starting with ...♕g4+, but ultimately the position is very difficult for Black.

63.♔e3 ♕e1+ 64.♔f4 ♕h4+ 65.♔xf5 ♕h5+ 66.♔e4 ♕e2+ 67.♔d4 ♕b2+ 68.♔d5 ♕b3+ 69.♔d6 ♕d3+ 70.♕d5 ♕g3+ 71.♔d7 ♕xa3

At this point, the engine announces mate in 15, starting with 72.♕d4+. But Fabi's technique is up to it.

72.e7 ♕a4+ 73.♔d8 ♕h4 74.♕c5+ ♔a6 75.♕e5 b5 76.♔d7 ♕h7 77.♔d6 ♕d3+ 78.♔c7 ♕h7 79.♔d8

We can only imagine the clock situation; 79.♕a1 mate would have been better.

79...♕h4 80.♕e6+ ♔a5 81.♔d7 ♕h7 82.♔c8 ♕c2+ 83.♔b7 ♕g2+ 84.♔b8 ♕h2+ 85.♔c8 ♕c2+ 86.♔b7 ♕g2+ 87.♕c6 ♕g7 88.♕c7+

Whew! Black resigned.

> In this game, Caruana taught me the force of sober resilience after having spoiled a huge opening advantage, and next solid endgame technique.

Here's a win by the same Grischuk with an opening he played several times in Paris.

**Alexander Grischuk
Ian Nepomniachtchi**
Paris 2019 (17)
King's Indian Defence

1.d4 ♘f6 2.c4 g6 3.h4

Although the first super-GM to play this in a serious game was Topalov in the 2016 Candidates against Giri, it seems Grischuk is serious about this experiment, which he first tried against MVL in the Riga Grand Prix. Let's wish Sasha all the best, as new ideas make chess a better game!

3...c6

Nepomniachtchi is a very pragmatic player when it comes to defending his favourite opening – the Grünfeld. Why play openings you don't play when you can play the openings you do play with an extra tempo? On the face of it, that may be true, but White has not fianchettoed his light-squared bishop, so he can use it better on the f1-a6 diagonal, and Black's ...g6 in the Slav cannot be much better than White's h4.

4.♘c3 d5 5.cxd5 cxd5 6.♗f4 ♗g7 7.e3 ♘c6

8.♗e2! An excellent move, securing White's comfort. Black will feel obliged to prepare for h5, meaning that Sasha just won back the tempo he lent Black on his third move.

8...h6 9.♘f3 ♗g4?

A serious mistake. Without the dark-squared bishop policing the d6-square, Black must keep his light-squared bishop in the defence. After 9...0-0 10.♖c1 ♕b6 11.♕b3! ♕xb3 12.axb3 ♗f5 13.♘e5 ♖fc8 14.g4 ♗e6 15.f3 White would have a slight pull, but now things can get ugly fast.

10.♕b3! ♘a5 The alternative was 10...♕b6 11.♕xb6 axb6 12.a3 0-0 13.♘e5 ♗xe2 14.♔xe2 ♖fc8 15.♖ac1 ♘a5 16.♘b5, with a serious positional endgame advantage for White.

11.♕a4+ ♗d7 12.♗b5

A strong alternative was 12.♕b4 or 12.♕a3, with serious pressure.

12...0-0?

Ian clearly doesn't like his position and decides to sacrifice a pawn to complete his development. This turns out to be simply bad, as Grischuk shows in a master class in technique. After the more tenacious 12...♘c6 13.♘e5 ♖c8 14.♗xc6 ♗xc6 15.♕xa7 0-0 16.0-0 ♘d7 17.♘xd7 ♕xd7

Let's wish Sasha all the best, as new ideas make chess a better game!

18.♕b6 Black's two bishops would provide some realistic compensation for the pawn, although of course only White would be trying to win.

13.♗xd7 ♘xd7 14.♘xd5 e5 15.dxe5 ♘xe5

16.♗xe5

With more time, it would have been possible to find a killer sequence: 16.♘xe5 ♕xd5 (16...♗xe5 17.♖d1!) 17.♖d1 ♕xg2 18.♖h2! ♕g1+ 19.♔e2, and the queen is lost.

16...♗xe5 17.♖d1 ♗g7 18.0-0 ♘c6 19.♖d2 ♕a5 20.♕xa5 ♘xa5 21.♖c1 ♖fd8 22.♘f1 ♔f8 23.b3 ♖ac8 24.♖xc8 ♖xc8 25.♔e2 ♖c1 26.♘b4 ♗f6 27.♖c2 ♖a1 28.g3 ♗e7 29.♘d5 ♘c6 30.♘d4 ♘xd4+ 31.exd4 ♗d6 32.♔d3 ♔e8 33.♖e2+ ♔d8 34.♘e3 ♗e7 35.♘g4

The knight is sent to systematically destroy Black's pawn structure.

35...h5 36.♘h6! f5 37.♘f7+ ♔d7 38.♘e5+ ♔c7 39.♘xg6 ♗d6 40.♘e7 f4 41.♘d5+ ♔c6 42.♘xf4 ♗xf4 43.gxf4 ♖h1 44.♖e6+ ♔d7 45.♖h6 ♖xh4 46.♔e4 ♖h1 47.f5 h4 48.♔e5 h3 49.♖h7+ ♔c6 50.f6 ♖e1+ 51.♔f5 ♖f1 52.f4

And Black had had enough.

In this game, Grischuk showed the nuances of his opening preparation, transposing to the Exchange Slav with Black's bishop on g7, while also winning a crucial tempo with 8.♗e2!. His endgame technique was also quite instructive, as he sent his knight to singlehandedly destroy and capture his opponent's pawns.

In the next game, Anish Giri was successful with a new idea, deviating in an opening line that has been seen many times. He beat Maxime Vachier-Lagrave, who was in poor blitz form, but still managed to take first place in the overall Rapid & Blitz standings and win 'Paris'.

Anish Giri
Maxime Vachier-Lagrave
Paris 2019 (15)
Sicilian Defence, Najdorf Variation

1.e4 c5 2.♘f3 d6 3.d4 cxd4
4.♘xd4 ♘f6 5.♘c3 a6 6.♗e3
♘g4 7.♗g5 h6 8.♗h4 g5 9.♗g3
♗g7 10.h3 ♘e5 11.♘f5 ♗xf5
12.exf5 ♘bc6 13.♘d5 e6 14.fxe6
fxe6 15.♘e3 ♕a5+ 16.c3

16...♘f3+ I found 219 games in the database in which Black played 16...♘f3+. Only in one game did White decide to double pawns with 17.gxf3. Amazingly enough, Anish Giri prepared a big surprise and repeated this move of correspondence player Dusan Poljak. That game ended in a draw, but when you face such a surprise in a blitz game, things may end badly for the recipient.

17.gxf3 To be fair, one of the key positions after 17.♕xf3 is pretty crazy as well: 17...♗xc3+ 18.♔d1 ♕a4+ 19.♘c2 ♗xb2 20.♖c1 ♖c8 21.♗d3 ♖f8 22.♕h5+ ♔d7 23.♕xh6 ♕xa2 24.♕h7+ ♘e7 25.♔e2 ♗xc1 26.♖xc1 ♕b2.

17...♗xc3+ 18.bxc3 ♕xc3+
19.♕d2 ♕xa1+ 20.♘d1 ♕d4
21.♗d3

21...♖f8
An official novelty and probably inaccurate. Black is not prepared to debate this complicated line fully.
In the afore-mentioned correspondence game Black played 21...♘e5, whereupon White captured on e5. I think it would have been interesting if Anish had tried 22.♗e2 instead, as in the endgame after 22...♕xd2+ 23.♔xd2 ♖c8 24.♘e3 ♗e7 25.f4 gxf4 26.♗xf4 ♖hf8 27.♗xh6 ♖xf2 28.♘g4 ♘xg4 29.hxg4, defending against the two bishops and the passed pawns could become tricky in a quick game.
22.0-0 ♖xf3 23.♘e3

White is down some material, but it's still quite hard to decide what to do with the black king here. Should Black castle or keep it in the middle? Tough choices for blitz.
23...♔d7 24.♖d1

Anish is eyeing the d6-square. Black's position is getting very dangerous.
24...♖af8
The best move, but one that took MVL 45 seconds.
25.♕e2

25...♕c5?
A tactical mistake. Black had some interesting options, but I think 25...♕c3 was probably the best. Then, after 26.♗e4 ♘d4 27.♕d2! ♖xg3+ 28.fxg3 ♕xd2 29.♖xd2 ♘c6, the three pawns would give Black hope for a successful defence.
26.♗e4 ♘d4?
This should have lost immediately. After the best continuation, 26...♖xg3+ 27.fxg3 ♕e5 28.♗g2 ♕xg3 29.♘g4 h5 30.♕b2 ♔c8 31.♖b1 ♖f7 32.♕h8+ ♘d8 33.♕xh5, White is much better with the queens still on the board.

Despite a 'horror show' (his words) in the blitz, MVL took overall first in Paris, much to the delight of Gilles Betthaeuser, the president of his sponsor Colliers.

LENNART OOTES

27.♕d3
Strong but not the best. After 27.♕b2! White's numerous threats will decide.
27...♖xg3+ 28.fxg3 e5?
With the queens on the board, Black has no chances. His last attempt was 28...♘c2 29.♕xc2 ♕xe3+ 30.♔g2 d5 31.♖d2, followed by ♖e2, and White is much better, although Black is still in the game.
29.♔g2 b5 30.♕d2 ♖c8 31.♘f5 ♕c3 32.♘xd4

Black resigned. Without his connected passed pawns he is hopelessly lost.

This game showed me the importance of analysing really rare lines in main openings and helped expand my understanding of knowing when to trade queens.

In the following game, Hikaru Nakamura shows his tenacity in bad positions, reversing his fortune after a failed attempt at aggression in the middlegame landed him into a piece-down fight with insufficient compensation.

Hikaru Nakamura
Anish Giri
Paris 2019 (14)
Sicilian Defence, Classical Variation
1.e4 c5 2.♘f3 d6 3.♘c3 ♘f6 4.h3 ♘c6 5.d4 cxd4
The somewhat rare move order 3.♘c3 and 4.h3 enabled Anish Giri to transpose to the 6.h3 variation of the Four Knights Sicilian. This should give Black an easier game.
6.♘xd4 e5

Hikaru tries to make the best out of a bad position by complicating as much as possible.

7.♘xc6 More usual is to try 7.♘de2, planning f4, although Black is fine in those lines as well.
7...bxc6 8.♗c4 ♗e7 9.0-0 0-0 10.♕e2 ♘d7 Anish decides against the natural 10...♗e6, planning to develop his bishop to a6.
11.♖d1 ♘b6 12.♗b3 12.♗a6 to trade off the light-squared bishop seems a tad better, as White's bishop on b3 is a bit out of play if Black sidesteps the pin on the f7-pawn with ...♔h8.
12...a5 13.♗e3 ♗a6 14.♕g4 ♔h8 15.f4? This natural move turns out to be a blunder, since it has opened the diagonal leading to the king, and White no longer has ♗xb6 as an option. White should have continued

reinforcing his position with 15.♖d2, or trying to create some kingside weaknesses with 15.♕h5.

15...a4! 16.fxe5
From this point on, Hikaru tries to make the best out of a bad position by complicating as much as possible.
16...♗c8? Already an inaccuracy. Anish does not need to misplace his bishop to win a piece, so he should simply have captured on b3, with a winning position.
After 16...axb3 17.exd6 ♗xd6 18.e5 Black had probably missed the retort 18...♘c4!, threatening the bishop and the e5-pawn.

17.♕f3? Hikaru misses his best chance. After 17.♕f4 axb3 18.exd6 bxc2 19.dxe7 cxd1♕+ 20.♖xd1 ♕xe7 21.♗xb6 ♗e6 22.b3 Black is much better, but there is a lot of work to do to convert the extra exchange.
17...axb3 18.cxb3 d5
Not obvious but more devastating for White would be repositioning the knight with 18...♘d7 19.exd6 ♘e5, followed by ...♗xd6, when White would hardly have any real compensation for the piece.
19.♕f2 ♖b8 20.♗xb6 ♕xb6

21.♕xb6 ♖xb6 22.exd5 cxd5 23.♘xd5

23...♖e6? A very dubious decision, as the two bishops provide additional power to Black's position. Keeping the bishop pair with 23...♗c5+ would have been decisive.

24.♘xe7 ♖xe7 25.♖d5 Suddenly White has three pawns on the queenside for the piece and Black has to start calculating how to stop them. Although Black is still winning here, let's see how fast his position falls apart.

25...♗e6 Another inaccuracy. The bishop belongs on b7 to make the e-pawn more accessible and to have an easier time blockading the oncoming queenside traffic.

26.♖b5 ♖d8 27.a4 g5 28.a5

28...♖d2? An outright blunder, after which Black is no longer better. The rooks had to be kept overseeing the pawns, the point being that White must not be allowed to play a6 and ♖aa5, since that would create a mechanism for White to continue pushing his pawns.

After the correct 28...♖a7, 29.b4 (29. a6 no longer works, because Black simply piles up on the pawn with ...♖da8 and ...♗c8) 29...♖d2! 30.♖b8+ ♔g7 31.b5 ♖c7! Black mounts a decisive attack before White has a chance to queen his pawns.

29.a6 ♖a7 30.♖b7 Besides 30.♖aa5, this is also good enough for equality.

30...♖d7? There was one nice way to equalize fully with 30...♖xg2+ 31.♔h1 ♗d5 32.♖xa7 ♖g3+ 33.♔h2 ♖g2+.

31.♖b8+? Missing the logical 31.♖xd7 ♗xd7 32.b4, when White will be a pawn up in a rook and pawn endgame after ♖a5 and b5. If Black tries to stop White's pawn advance with ...♗c8, White will reposition his rook, with excellent winning chances.

31...♔g7 32.b4 ♗c4 33.b5

33...♖d2? In time-pressure, it proved impossible to find 33...♖d5 34.♖a5 ♖d1+ 35.♔h2 ♖d2 36.e6 fxe6 37.♖b7+ ♖xb7 38.axb7 ♗d5 39.b8♕ ♖xg2+ 40.♔h1 ♖g3+, with a draw.

34.b3!? This move gives Black a chance to go wrong, but he should draw with best play. 33.♖a4 seemed stronger, but I was able to find a draw for Black in

all variations. I welcome you to try and analyse the position yourself!

34...♗e2?? The final mistake. For some reason, Anish decides to control the pawns by keeping the bishop on the a6-f1 diagonal, missing a neat tactic. After 34...♗d5 (the only move) 35.b6 ♖xg2+ 36.♔f1 ♖d7! Black's counter-play of posting both rooks on the second rank with a perpetual cannot be stopped. For example: 37.b7 ♗xb7 38.axb7 ♖dd2 39.♖g8+ ♔h6!.

35.e6! The opening of the seventh rank decides the game.

35...♖b2 36.♖b7 ♖a8 37.♖xf7+ ♔g6 38.♖f2!

1-0. A cute finishing touch. Hikaru simply restricts all Black's pieces. The pawn onslaught cannot be stopped.

This game taught me an attractive opening plan with ♘xc6 and ♗c4 that may give White a little pull in slightly different positions from what a Sicilian player is used to. The fight of the pawns against the bishop was also very instructive, because Black's strongest counters always focused on White's king, rather than on blocking play against the pawns. ■

The good, the beautiful and the ugly

Flights of fancy, sound endgame advice or 'dark-square weakness hooliganism'. You'll find them all as **MATTHEW SADLER** gives you a taste of a rich harvest of new books.

Some months ago (in New In Chess 2019/4) I wrote that I hadn't dared pick up Oleg Pervakov's *Industrial Strength Endgame Studies* by Sergei Tkachenko (Elk and Ruby) before a tournament lest I depress myself by failing to solve them! However, since my chess activity is pretty much completed for the rest of this year, I thought I might have a go! Oleg Pervakov was born in the Russian city of Kirov in 1960 and published his first composition in 1977. After a gap of a few years, he returned to composition in 1983 and was immediately successful, sharing first prize in a competition together with no other than Kasparian. This book brings together 100 of Pervakov's best studies. The blurb at the back says that you may buy this collection of studies 'to test your endgame tactical abilities, to improve your endgame understanding, or simply to appreciate chess in all its beauty'. I strained for a while at the first but then settled with great – though

slightly guilty – satisfaction into the third reason! And indeed, treating this book as an art book, dipping into it from time to time to marvel at the miracles that Pervakov weaves with the pieces, has proven to be a great pleasure.

During the recent Dutch Championship, at a Deloitte sponsor's event at which Natasha Regan and I were talking about AlphaZero, the Dutch IM Manuel Bosboom came along and demonstrated a series of amazing positions (very impressively from memory) with stunning resources for both sides. I think he would enjoy these very much! Pervakov says that he likes studies with 'a battle between the two sides, tricks they can come up with. So it has to be a battle of equals. It's just like when two players of the same strength meet

over the board and each has a set of aces up his sleeve'. It's this feeling of amazing ingenuity on both sides that makes his studies very appealing to practical players. For example, I loved the elegance of this study that I could easily imagine coming up in a blitz finish!

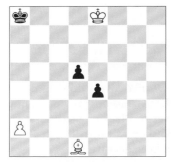

O. Pervakov & N. Kralin
64 Chess Review 1995
White to play and win

Black's two connected passed pawns threaten to slowly walk down to the first rank. How can the white bishop outplay them?
1.♔d7 d4 2.♗b3 e3 3.♗c4 ♔b7 4.♔d6 ♔b6 5.♔d5 ♔a5

6.♔e4 Aaaah! 6.♔xd4 ♔b4 is zugzwang! 7.♔d3 e2.
6...♔a4 7.♔d3 ♔a3 7...♔b4 8.♔xd4 wins! **8.♔c2 e2 9.♔d2 d3 10.♔e1 ♔b2 11.a4 ♔c3 12.♗xd3 ♔xd3 13.a5** Wonderful!

Dipping into the book to marvel at the miracles that Pervakov weaves with the pieces, has proven to be a great pleasure.

At the other end of the scale, there are mind-boggling flights of fantasy like this one!

O. Pervakov
64 Chess Review 2005
White to play and win

1.♕c1+ ♗d1 1...♔xf2 2.♘h3+ ♔e2 3.♘f4+ ♔f2 4.♕g1 mate. **2.♘xd1 ♖xd2+** 2...cxd1♕ 3.♕xd1+ ♔f2 4.♕e2 mate. **3.♘f2+ ♖d1** 3...♔xf2 4.♕xd2+ ♔f1 5.♕e2 mate.

... and now(!): **4.♘d3 ♖xc1 5.♘e2**

Amazing!! 6.♘g3 mate is threatened and... **5...♔xe2 6.♘xc1+ ♔d2 7.♘xa2** wins the house!

In summary, a wonderful treasure-trove of exquisitely beautiful ideas!

Oleg Pervakov's Industrial Strength Endgame Studies by Sergei Tkachenko Elk and Ruby, 2019
★★★★★

If you're brave enough to solve them, then it will certainly improve your calculation. If you're just lazy like me, then you'll have an even better time playing through them! 5 stars!

■ ■ ■

From all that is beautiful in chess to all that is ugliest: the French Winawer Defence! *The Modernized French Defence* by David Miedema (Thinkers Publishing) is a bright and cheerful book full of ideas, double exclamation mark novelties and... weak dark squares!

After reading through this book, I had to go and play through some Najdorf games just to remind myself that horrific holes aren't always necessary. Note that although it isn't completely clear from the title, this is not a complete French repertoire book, as the coverage starts from 1.e4 e6 2.d4 d5 3.♘c3 ♗b4. Miedema cites Moskalenko's excellent, idiosyncratic works on the French (*The Wonderful Winawer* – New In Chess, 2010) a few times and indeed Miedema's book has a similar feel to those: lots of analysis, maybe sometimes a touch too much enthusiasm for rather dodgy-looking ideas, but nevertheless a stimulating read when you want to get some out-of-the-box inspiration in your favourite opening.

I suppose the line that most shocked me was this recommendation against the 7.a4 line against the Winawer.
1.e4 e6 2.d4 d5 3.♘c3 ♗b4 4.e5 ♘e7 5.a3 ♗xc3+ 6.bxc3 c5 7.a4 ♕c7

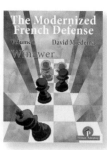

The Modernized French Defence by David Miedema Thinkers Publishing, 2019
★★★★☆

Miedema explains that he had poor results against 7.a4, but 'Then I had to go into my study-cave for a few days, hardly eating, renouncing all of life's pleasures, just a flat-out threesome with Stockfish, Komodo and me. But I found enlightenment, The Answer, not exactly to Life, The Universe and Everything, but at least to Black's worries in this line.'
8.♘f3 h6 9.♗b5+ ♗d7 10.♗d3 ♘bc6 11.0-0 c4 12.♗e2 a5 13.♗a3 b5 14.axb5 ♘a7 15.b6 ♕xb6 16.♗c5 ♕d8

Pretty odd play. Miedema points out that Morozevich played a similar idea (starting with 10...c4 and 11...a5) but lost in 26 moves in rather brutal fashion... The plan is ...a4, ...♘b5 and ....♕a5. You must be real hard-core Winawer material to want to play this!

But I mustn't let my anti-Winawer prejudices influence me too much! There is plenty of interesting material to enjoy. But just keep your healthy scepticism switched on before trying out some of the more exotic ideas! Somewhere between 3 and 4 stars. I'll be generous and bump it up to 4!

■ ■ ■

After being exposed to this dark-square weakness hooliganism, it seemed quite appropriate to start on a book called *Say No to Chess Principles!* by Evgeny Bareev (Thinkers Publishing). Also very appropriately, the very last game of the book features the same variation of the French... and even quotes the Oparin-Morozevich game, claiming a slight advantage for Black after 15 moves! So, what do I know!?

The book is a collection of 55 games from Bareev's illustrious career, organised in thematic chapters, each dedicated to an illustration of a general principle that didn't hold true! For example, we have chapters on 'Play without castling', 'When a piece in the centre is grim', 'At the edge of the board' and 'Rewards of doubled pawns'. Bareev's annotations are his typical mix of irony, forthright opinions on fellow players and excellent chess instruction which make it both an enjoyable read and a very interesting source of unusual chess knowledge. As I get a little older, I notice that my pleasure in playing through lots of variations has decreased significantly and that I am much keener on evocative examples of themes, and this book is full of them. For example, take these two examples from the chapter 'When a piece in the centre is grim'. I've pinned them into my memory!

Jan Timman
Evgeny Bareev
Wijk aan Zee 2002
English Opening, Reversed Sicilian

1.c4 e5 2.♘c3 ♘f6 3.♘f3 ♘c6 4.g3 ♗c5 5.♗g2 0-0 6.♘xe5 ♗xf2+ 7.♔xf2 ♘xe5 8.b3 ♖e8 9.♖f1 d5 10.d4 ♘eg4+ 11.♔g1 dxc4 12.bxc4 ♘e3 13.♗xe3 ♖xe3 14.♕d2 ♖e8 15.♖ad1 c6 16.♕f4 ♗g4 17.♖f2 ♗h5 18.d5

This was the plan. White is under the wrong impression about the d5-outpost and the dividends it will bring. His impressions are usually correct, just not in this case.
18...cxd5 19.♘xd5 ♘g4

20.♖ff1 Maybe it was worth playing 20.♘e3 (giving up the occupation of the d5-square White fought so hard to achieve! – MS) 20...♘xe3 21.♖xd8 ♖axd8 22.♗d5 ♘xd5 23.cxd5 ♖xd5 24.♕a4 b5 25.♕xa7 ♖de5, though

Black certainly looks better there.
20...♘e5

Unbelievably, all of Timman's pieces are worthless! The centralized knight limits the scope of the bishop and one rook, while the queen and the other rook aren't doing anything on the f-file. On top of that, his pawn structure is ruined. Such was the price of the d5-outpost – it seems as though it cost too much.
21.♕c1 A miscalculation. It was necessary to admit the plan's failure, trade the knight and thereby activate his other pieces: 21.♕f2 ♗g6 22.♘f4 ♕c7 23.♘d5 with an equal position.
21...♗xe2 22.♘f6+ gxf6 23.♖xd8 ♖axd8 Black has a material and positional advantage.

24.♗xb7 ♔g7 25.♗d5 ♗xf1 26.♕xf1 ♖b8 27.♕f2 ♘d3 28.♕xa7 ♖e1+ 29.♔g2 ♖b2+ 30.♔h3 ♘e5 31.g4 ♖ee2 32.♔g3 ♖xa2 33.♕c5 ♖ad2 0-1.

It's interesting to compare these annotations with the mainly symbol comments by Ftacnik and Ribli in ChessBase: you just don't get the same impression of the game at all. That's the power of a strong player explaining

Bareev's annotations are his typical mix of irony, forthright opinions on fellow players and excellent chess instruction.

his own games to you, as well as the value of organising material thematically. The lessons to be learnt from a game just jump out at you so much better.

Evgeny Bareev
Christopher Lutz
Turin Olympiad 2006
Queen's Indian, Petrosian Variation

1.d4 ♘f6 2.c4 e6 3.♘f3 b6 4.♘c3 ♗b7 5.a3 d5 6.cxd5 ♘xd5 7.e3 ♗e7 8.♗b5+ c6 9.♗d3 0-0 10.0-0 ♘xc3 11.bxc3 c5 12.♕e2 ♘d7 13.e4 ♕c7 14.♗b2 ♖ac8 15.♘d2 ♕f4 16.♖ad1 cxd4 17.cxd4 ♖fd8 18.e5 b5 19.♘e4

19...♘b6 Chess is like running in circles: first you learn to defend your pawns, then to sacrifice them. But you finally learn when to defend them and when to sacrifice them.

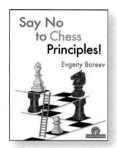

Say No to Chess Principles!
by Evgeny Bareev
Thinkers Publishing, 2019
★★★★★

At this point a relatively calm defence suggests itself: 19...a6 20.a4 bxa4 21.♖a1 ♘b6 22.g3 ♕h6 23.h4 g6 24.♗xa6 ♗xa6 25.♕xa6 ♖b8.
20.g3 ♕h6 21.♗xb5 g6 22.a4 ♕f8 23.a5 ♗xe4 24.♕xe4 ♘d5

This is the crowning achievement of the career of the knight: an outpost on d5.
25.a6 ♗a3 26.♗a1 ♗b4 27.♖b1 ♗c3 Lutz decides to bet it all on the knight which will ultimately end up being lame. In reality, the problem could have been solved mathemati-

cally after the forcing 27...♘c3 (again exchanging off the central piece that Black has spent so much time establishing! – MS) 28.♗xc3 ♗xc3 29.♖fd1 ♖d5 30.♔g2 ♖cd8 31.♗c6 ♖xd4 32.♖xd4 ♖xd4.
28.♖b3 ♗xa1 29.♖xa1 ♖c3 30.♖ab1

As it turns out, the knight is practically – though temporarily – out of moves. Worse, White can exchange it whenever he wants, and he will.
30...♕h6 31.♗f1 ♖cc8 32.♖b7 ♕f8 33.♕h4 ♖b8 34.♖1b3 ♖dc8 35.♕g5 ♖xb7 36.axb7 ♖b8 37.♕c1 a5 38.♖b5 ♔g7 39.♗g2 a4 40.♗xd5 exd5 41.♕c6 ♕a3 42.♕f6+ ♔g8 43.♖c5 1-0.

All-in-all, some really good insights from a very strong player! 5 stars!

■ ■ ■

Finally, we move back from the realm of fantasy and broken rules to the logical austerity of king and pawn endgames! I reviewed an earlier edition of *Liquidation on the Chess Board* by Joel Benjamin (New In Chess) a couple of years ago – extremely favourably judging from the blurb on the back! – and it goes without saying that I am still of the same opinion. This edition adds 50 new examples and incorporates some corrections and analysis by a more recent analysis engine.

The book addresses the topic of when to liquidate from an ending with several pieces into a pawn endgame. It's obviously an important topic for good endgame play, but it doesn't really sound like a thrilling or rich subject: that was certainly my initial reaction. However, the inherent complexity of pawn endings continually throws up startling twists and turns in the games. After reading the book, I'm more than a little nervous of looking through such liquidation examples in my own games: who knows how many mistakes I have made! The difficulty with king and pawn endgames is that calculation plays a huge role from the moment you enter them, and that steering just on positional logic is asking for disaster. Take this rather tragic example!

Viktor Kortchnoi
Jordi Magem Badals
Pamplona 1994/95

position after 47...h6

White has no obligation to lose. He can hardly lose after 48.♔d3 c5

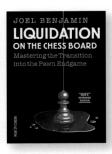
49.♔c4 ♔e7 50.♗b1. But the pawn ending can be calculated to a draw.
48.a4
48.♗xe6+ ♔xe6 49.♔xd4 c5+ 50.♔xc5 ♔xe5 51.♔b5 ♔f4 52.♔a6 ♔xg4 53.♔xa7 h5 54.a4 h4 55.a5 h3 56.a6 h2 57.♔b8 h1♛ 58.a7 (I imagine that Kortchnoi saw this draw but decided to give himself some extra leeway by already advancing his a-pawn closer to the queening square. It sounds sensible and logical... – MS).
48...♔e7 49.♗xe6 ♔xe6 50.♔xd4 a5

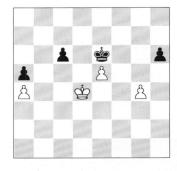

And White resigned as 51.♔c5 ♔xe5 52.♔xc6 ♔f4 53.♔b5 ♔xg4 54.♔xa5 h5 55.♔b6 h4 56.a5 h3 57.a6 h2 58.a7 h1♛ wins!

Advancing your pawn two moves closer to the queening square made it slower to queen! Doesn't sound fair, but that's pawn endings for you, when having waiting pawn moves in reserve is often more important than the speed with which you advance them! All in all, a valuable and very enjoyable book to read! I think I gave it 4 stars before, let's go for 5 this time! ■

Jan Timman

Prodigious Pragga

The Xtracon Open ended in a sensational victory for 13-year-old Rameshbabu Praggnanandhaa. Seeded 21st the Indian prodigy was ruthless with White and solid with Black. **JAN TIMMAN** reports and tests the reader's tactical skills with a set of puzzles from Helsingor.

A shadow hung over the Xtracon Open in Helsingor this year: Lars Bech Hansen, the great organizer of the tournament, had died just under a month before the start. His death was a real blow for me. I had known Lars for many years as an amiable man with an enormous capacity for work; always busy, but always making time for a friendly conversation. I remember a situation from two years ago. Ivan Sokolov was giving a lecture, and he asked Lars whether he would be there. 'I would love to, but I have too much work to do,' Lars replied. 'But don't you have a back-up?' Ivan asked. The reply: 'I am my back-up'. This characterized Lars to a T – he didn't delegate.

His death is a great loss to Danish chess; he also organized the Danish championship. He took out a lot of time for the Helsingor tournament, both for organizing the event and for running it. His wife Dorte and daughter Christine were always involved in the organization as well, and they were there again this year.

Three additional arbiters had been hired, and IM Jacob Carstensen acted as tournament director. A compliment is in order here: not only did the tournament run its customarily solid course, but the dates for next year's event have already been set.

There were no 2700+ players in Helsingor this time, but the Elo-favourites had been at that level earlier: Grandelius, Korobov and Sargissian, to mention just a few big shots. None of them managed to win the tournament, though. Final victory was claimed by 13-year-old Rameshbabu Praggnanandhaa, who was seeded 21st. I have already written about the Indian phenomenon in New In Chess, before he secured his grandmaster title. The question then was whether he would become the youngest GM of all time. He didn't, but this is not really important. Nor does it matter that he seemed to stagnate for a while. These are common occurrences in the lives of young super-talents; sooner or later, the breakthrough will come. For Praggnanandhaa it came in Helsingor: his 8½ out of 10 score yielded him 29 rating points.

An important win for him was his sixth-round game against Korobov.

Anton Korobov
Rameshbabu Praggnanandhaa
Helsingor 2019 (6)

position after 44...♗a2

Is it possible that something is still going to happen in this bishop ending? The players could easily have signed the peace here. But Korobov has one more thing to try.
45.a4 A step in the wrong direction, but the equilibrium has not yet been broken.
45...a5 Of course. Black creates a dangerous passed a-pawn.
46.axb5 ♔xb5

47.♗g6?? A terrible blunder. Called for was 47.♗d3+ to keep the black a-pawn in check.
47...a4 48.♗d3+ ♔a5

I assume Korobov had overlooked that this square was now available to the king. This is a well-known sign of tiredness: forgetting that moving a piece or a pawn vacates a square.
49.♔e3 a3 50.♔d2 ♗b3 51.♔c1 ♔b6 White resigned.

After this win the young Indian admirably stuck to his schedule: winning as White and drawing as Black. His style struck me as very technical, as witness, for example, this victory in Round 7.

**Rameshbabu Praggnanandhaa
Daniele Vocaturo**
Helsingor 2019 (7)
Sicilian Defence, Accelerated Dragon

**1.e4 c5 2.♘f3 g6 3.d4 cxd4
4.♘xd4 ♘c6 5.c4 ♘f6 6.♘c3 d6
7.♗e2 ♘xd4 8.♕xd4 ♗g7 9.♗e3
0-0 10.♕d2 a5 11.f3 a4 12.♔f2**

A remarkable move not unknown to chess practice. White does not castle, because he is preparing for an endgame.
12...♕a5 13.♖ac1 ♗e6 14.♘d5
The consequence of the 12th move.
14...♗xd5 15.♕xa5 It is important to swap the queens; otherwise, Black might operate on the c-file.
15...♖xa5 16.cxd5 ♘d7
Vocaturo is going to take his knight to c5 in order to throw up a strong defence. The alternative was 16...e6, opening the centre. After 17.♗f4

Another milestone. In Helsingor 'Pragga' won his first major international tournament at the tender age of 13 years and 11 months.

exd5 18.♗xd6 ♖e8, Black has reasonable counterplay.
17.♖c7 ♘c5 18.♖b1 ♗f6

19.b4
Schematic play. Probably stronger would have been to attack on the other wing with 19.g4. After 19...g5

20.h4 h6 21.hxg5 hxg5 22.♖h1, White is better.
19...axb3 20.axb3 ♖a2 21.b4 ♘a4 22.♖bc1 ♖b2 23.♗h6 ♗g7 24.♗xg7 ♔xg7 25.♖xe7 ♖xb4 26.♖cc7 g5 Black sacrifices his b-pawn to keep his defensive line intact. Had he gone 26...b6, White could have increased the pressure with 27.♖c6 ♖d8 28.f4 ♘c5 29.♗f3, and the e-pawn advances powerfully.

In the lives of young super-talents, sooner or later, the breakthrough will come.

27.e5!

A strong breakthrough, especially from a practical point of view. Black will have to solve some difficult problems in time-trouble.

27.♖xb7 would probably have been objectively better here, but after 27...♖xb7 28.♖xb7 ♘c5 29.♖b6 ♖d8, Black has a less complicated job defending.

27...dxe5 28.d6 ♖d4 29.♗c4 ♖xd6 30.♗xf7 ♔f6 31.♗h5 ♖c6 32.♖xb7 ♘c5

Just falling short. With 32...♖c2+ 33.♔g3 ♘c3 Black could have created sufficient counterplay. White has no realistic winning chances.

33.♖f7+ ♖xf7 34.♗xf7+ ♔e6 35.♗xh7 ♘d3+ 36.♔e3 ♖c3

36...♘b4 37.♗g4+ ♔f6 would have offered better chances of a successful defence. White would have found it hard to make progress.

37.♖h6+ ♔e7 38.♔e4 ♘f4

39.g3! Praggnanandhaa has spotted that this gives White a winning rook ending.

39...♘xh5 40.♖xh5 ♔f6 41.♖h6+ ♔f7 42.♖d6 ♖c2 43.♔xe5 ♖xh2 44.♔f5 ♖h3 45.♔g4

Black resigned.

Test Yourself

The following five exercises are based on actual game positions from the 2019 Xtracon Open. The solutions are given at the end of this article on page 97.

Things nearly came unstuck for Praggnanandhaa in the final round, in which he was squaring up to a young star from a different continent, American talent Samuel Sevian, as Black. Sevian had lost against 18-year-old Indian WGM Vaishali (Praggnanandhaa's sister!) in an earlier round, and now he could make up for it. The two of them sitting at the board made for a curious spectacle, with Sevian looking about three times the size of the young Indian. And Sevian nearly managed to secure tournament victory, only to let the win slip through his fingers deep into the endgame.

**Samuel Sevian
Rameshbabu Praggnanandhaa**
Helsingor 2019 (10)

position after 64...♕d6

Almost all games had finished when this position arose. White needs to find a square for his queen.

65.♕e4+

The wrong one! With 65.♕c4! White could have won, ending up with an elementary pawn ending. The main line goes as follows: 65...♕c7 66.h5 ♔d6 67.♔h3 ♕xc6 68.♕xc6+ ♔xc6 69.♔g4 ♔d6 70.♔f5 ♔e7 71.♔g6 ♔f8 72.h6 gxh6 73.♔xf6, and wins.

65...♔d8 66.♕h7 ♕xc6 67.♕g8+ ♔e8 68.♕xg7 ♕e2+ 69.♔h3 ♕f1+ 70.♔g4 ♕e2+ 71.♔h3 ♕f1+ 72.♔g4 ♕e2+ 73.♔h3 Draw.

The brilliancy prize – put up by New In Chess – went to 26-year-old Kassa Korley, who also scored a grandmaster result. His win over Moiseenko was indeed spectacular.

**Alexander Moiseenko
Kassa Korley**
Helsingor 2019 (4)
Queen's Gambit Declined,
Exchange Variation

1.d4 d5 2.c4 e6 3.♘c3 ♘f6 4.cxd5 exd5 5.♗g5 c6 6.e3 ♗d6 7.♗d3 0-0 8.♕c2 h6 9.♗h4 ♖e8 10.♘ge2 a5 11.h3 ♘a6 12.a3 ♘c7 13.0-0 ♘e6 14.f3 ♘g5

Exercise 1

Kryakvin-Ask (2)
position after 17.♖g2

Black sacrificed a piece here with
17...♘b3+ 18.axb3 axb3
How should White have defended?

Exercise 2

Ivarsson-Cramling (2)
position after 32.♗f3

Pia Cramling wanted to win here and went for **32...♕xb5?** How could White have exploited this?

Korley played remarkably fast. Had he prepared everything?

15.e4? Obvious, thematic – and losing! White should have advanced the other pawn: 15.f4, with slightly better play. Black can sacrifice a piece by 15...♘xh3+ 16.gxh3 ♖xe3, but after 17.♗f5 he doesn't have full compensation.

15...♘fxe4! The start of a magnificent combination.

16.fxe4 ♘xh3+! The point of the previous move. Black will end up with three pawns and a strong attack for the piece.

17.gxh3 ♕xh4 18.♖f2 ♗xh3 19.♖d1

19...♖e5!! The *coup de grâce*. The rook offer is the most convincing way to crown the attack. But the prosaic 19...dxe4 20.♘xe4 ♗c7 21.♕b3 ♖e6 would also have won.

20.dxe5 ♗c5 21.♘d4 ♗xd4 22.♖dd2 ♕g3+ 23.♔h1 ♗g4 24.♗f1 ♗f3+ 25.♔g2 ♕h3+

White resigned.

Korley played remarkably fast. Had he prepared everything? There turned out to be a different reason: he had already executed this combination last March. All the thinking had been done then!

Tanguy Ringoir
Kassa Korley
Charlotte 2019
Queen's Gambit Declined, Exchange Variation

1.d4 d5 2.c4 e6 3.♘c3 ♘f6 4.cxd5 exd5 5.♗g5 c6 6.e3 ♗d6 7.♗d3 h6 8.♗h4 0-0 9.♘ge2 ♖e8 10.h3 a5 11.♕c2 ♘a6 12.a3 ♘c7 13.0-0 ♘e6 14.♖ad1 ♗d7 15.f3 ♘g5

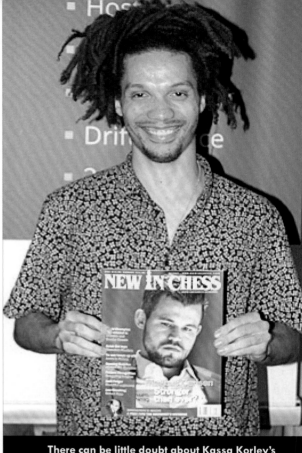

Exercise 3

Hjartarson-Tari (7)
position after 24...♔h8

Black seems to be strategically strong, but White has a way to secure a large advantage. What should he play?

Exercise 4

Timman-Thaler (7)
position after 13.♖d1

Instead of playing his queen, Black went **13...a5 14.♕c5 ♘fd7** How could White have exploited this?

Exercise 5

Vesterli-Christiansen (9)
position after 15.d5

In the Moscow Variation White has just advanced his d-pawn. Black must take on e5. Which piece should he use?

The situation is slightly different here, because ♖a1-d1 and ♗c8-d7 have been played, which makes the situation after Black's sacrifices slightly less disastrous for White; he has a tempo more.

16.e4 Here, 16.f4 would have been correct, too, although Black would get sufficient compensation for the

piece after 16...♘xh3+ 17.gxh3 ♖xe3 18.♗f5 ♕c8! 19.♗xd7 ♕xd7.

16...♘fxe4 17.fxe4 ♘xh3+ 18.gxh3 ♕xh4 19.♖f2 ♗xh3 20.e5

20...♖xe5! Again that rook sac. But now White no longer has an e-pawn, which, paradoxically, improves his chances of a successful defence.

21.dxe5 ♗c5 22.♘d4 ♗xd4 23.♗h7+

This explains why the lack of a pawn on e4 works to White's advantage.

23...♔h8 24.♖xd4 ♕xd4 25.♕d3

White has done all he could defensively, but Black would have kept a large plus if he had taken on e5. However, he checked the white king on g4 instead, diluting his advantage.

25...♕g4+ 26.♔h2 ♕h4 27.♕g3 ♕xg3+ 28.♔xg3 ♗xh7 29.♔xh3 ♔g8 30.♘a4 ♖e8 31.♘c5 ♖e7 32.♖c2 b6 33.♘a4 b5 34.♘b6 ♖xe5 35.♖xc6 ♖e2 36.b4 ♖e3+ 37.♔g4 axb4 38.axb4 ♖e4+ 39.♔f3 ♖xb4 40.♘xd5 ♖c4 41.♖b6 ♖c5 42.♔e4 h5 43.♔d4 ♖c4+ 44.♔e3 b4 45.♘xb4 ♖c3+ 46.♘d3 ♖c7 47.♘f4 g6 48.♘xg6 Draw.

Moiseenko should not really have missed that game in his preparation. And there was another thing: the first 18 moves of Moiseenko-Korley had occurred in the Russian Championship more than 20 years ago. In Karpeshov-Meister, Perm 1997, White continued 19.e5, after which he was trailing Ringoir by a full tempo. Black made the now well-known sacrifice and was clearly winning. Yet this game, too, ended in a draw.

■ ■ ■

Halfway the tournament, I gave a lecture on my book *The Longest Game*, which was well attended and successful, something that could not really be said about my tournament.

The lecture gave me the chance to make some minor rectifications. Important was the assessment of the endgame of Game 2 in the second match of the two Ks.

Anatoly Karpov
Garry Kasparov
Moscow second match 1985 (2)

position after 47.♔f2

This is the position I want to show you. Kasparov now went:

47...h5

In my comments in New In Chess 1985/11, I put a question mark after this advance, observing that Black could have won with 47...♖e5 48.g4 ♖e4. Kasparov disputes this assessment in *Kasparov vs Karpov*, Part 2, giving a pretty long variation and concluding that White would have had 'real saving chances'. Since I thought that the final position of

Sorokhtin is a carpenter from St. Petersburg who has been critically following Kasparov's analyses for years.

that line was a dead draw, I decided to restrict myself in *The Longest Game* to the brief comment that the black rook cannot penetrate. Such are the practical decisions you sometimes have to take when writing a lengthy book – there had been so many interesting moments in this game, and I had already so often disputed Kasparov's assessment. In February, New In Chess received a mail from Sergey Sorokhtin telling me that my original assessment had been correct after all. Sorokhtin is a carpenter from St. Petersburg who has been critically following Kasparov's analyses for years. In 2004, ChessBase published a number of his conclusions on Part I of *My Great Predecessors*. Sorokhtin had spent days analysing the endgame of Game 2 with the help of Stockfish 10, concluding that Black was winning. The main line went as follows: 49.♗d2 ♖c4 50.♗c3 a3 51.♔g3 h5 52.gxh5,

ANALYSIS DIAGRAM

and now Black must go 52...♔h7! (instead of Kasparov's 52...♖e4, when 53.♔f3 leads to a draw). White has no

defence: 53.f6 (or 53.♗b4 ♖d4!) 53... gxf6 54.♗xf6 ♔h6, and Black has a technically winning position.

ANALYSIS DIAGRAM

There are a few more possible lines, but it remains a fact that Kasparov could have made sure of this game. **48.♗c3 ♖b8 49.♗b4 ♖d8 50.♔e2 a3 51.♗c3 f6 52.♗b4 ♔f7 53.♘c3 ♖b8 54.♘a2 ♖b5 55.g4 ♖b8 56.♔d3 ♖d8+ 57.♔c4 ♖d1 58.♗xa3 ♖a1 59.♔b3 ♖h1 60.gxh5 ♖xh3+ 61.♘c3 ♖f3 62.♗c1 ♖xf5 63.h6 g6 64.♘e4 ♖h5 65.♗b2** Draw.

The escape in this game had been of crucial importance to Karpov – otherwise he would have lost four games on the trot: the last two games of the first match and the first two of the second one. ∎

Solutions

Exercise 1

White should have gone 19.♘b1! instead of 19.♘fe4, as in the game, because in reply to this move 19...♘f6! would have been strong and White will find it hard to withstand the pressure along the b1-h7 diagonal. After 20.♗d3 ♖a1+ 21.♘b1 ♘xe4 22.fxe4 ♗xe4 23.♖hg1 ♗xg2 24.♕xg2 ♗h6 Black has excellent play.
After withdrawing the knight to b1 he would be fine, as witness: 19...♖a1 (otherwise White would block the

a-file by playing his knight to a3) 20.♘e4 ♘f6 21.♘ec3 and White has organized his defence.

Exercise 2

With 33.♖b1 White could have won. Not 33.♖ed1??, as in the game, which ran into 33...♘xf3 34.♖xd8+ ♗xd8 35.♖xd8+ ♔h7, and Black was winning because 36.♔xf3 would fail to 36...♕c6+.
With the rook on b1, Black has no defence, since 33...♘b3 would fail to 34.♖dxb3 axb3 35.♖xb3 and the black bishop would be lost.

Exercise 3

Very strong was 25.♘g3!. If Black now advances his f-pawn, White has secured all strategic trump cards. But there is little choice, because 25...e4 would fail to 26.♘xe4! fxe4 27.♕xe4 and there is no defence against the mating threat on h7. It is not difficult, but you have to spot the idea. Hjartarson played his rook to g1, cementing Black's position.

Exercise 4

With 15.♖xd7! White could have won material. I didn't play it, because it looks as if Black would surround the white queen after 15...♗xd7 16.♕xb6 ♗d4, when White has the elegant check 17.♗d5+!, keeping his material plus. In the game, I withdrew my queen to a3; real proof of bad form.

Exercise 5

His best bet is 15...♘xe5. If White then captures on e6, the knight can go to d3.
The game saw 15...♗xe5 16.dxe6 ♗xd6 17.♕xd6 ♘f6 18.♕e5! ♕e7, and now 19.f4! (instead of 19.♗h5) would have been very strong. The black fortress will be smashed, e.g. 19...♕xe6 20.♕xe6+ fxe6 21.fxg5 ♘d5 22.♗h5+ ♔d8 23.g6, with a winning advantage.

Simen Agdestein

CURRENT ELO: **2560**

DATE OF BIRTH: **May 15, 1967**

PLACE OF BIRTH: **Oslo, Norway**

PLACE OF RESIDENCE: **Oslo, Norway**

What is your favourite city?
Oslo, with the fjord on the lower side, lots of green spots and only 20 minutes on the tube to the forest with lakes.

What was the last great meal you had?
I normally care more about the company than the food.

What drink brings a smile to your face?
Fresh orange juice is fine with me.

Which book would you give to a friend?
Normally the last book I manage to read I want everyone else to read too.

What is your all-time favourite movie?
Grease, with John Travolta and Olivia Newton John at their best. Very cool!

And your favourite TV series?
Breaking bad and the Swedish comedies *Solsidan* (The Sunny Side) and *Bonusfamiljen* (Bonus Family) are fantastic.

What music do you listen to?
Currently, it's piano jazz.

Is there a painting that moves you?
I can be just as moved by a loving pic on the phone as by a great piece of art.

Who is your favourite player of all time?
I grew up with Karpov, Kortchnoi and Kasparov, but I consider my former pupil Magnus Carlsen to be the very best player of all time.

Is there a chess book that had a profound influence on you?
The Middle Game by Max Euwe was my first book. Kasparov's books on his predecessors are fantastic reading, but the analyses are way above my level.

What was your best result ever?
Hastings 1991/92 was the last good tournament in a streak of good results. Since then it's been totally random.

And the best game you played?
Perhaps my win against Speelman in 1991.

What is your favourite square?
Solid and in the middle, d4. I like fighting for the centre right away.

Do chess players have typical shortcomings?
Plenty! Spending so much time on just a game has a price.

What are chess players particularly good at (except for chess)?
We are good at being ourselves. No boring stereotypes in the chess world!

Facebook, Instagram, Snapchat, or?
I see obvious marketing reasons for being active on social media, but I dislike bragging and barely dare to post anything on Facebook.

How many friends do you have on Facebook?
1466. It's good to have them all there, but I don't communicate with many.

Who do you follow on Twitter?
A few, but I never check, so in fact no one.

What is your life motto?
In real life? Perhaps 'You can learn something from everyone'.

When were you happiest?
When I decided to stop playing chess full-time at 21 and enrolled in university and returned to soccer. I was so inspired that I made the national Norwegian soccer team that autumn.

When was the last time you cried?
The last 15 minutes of *Bohemian Rhapsody*. The music, the story, the effects; it all worked on me!

Who or what would you like to be if you weren't yourself?
An amateur sport maniac with no injuries.

Which three people would you like to invite for dinner?
My first childhood love, if one. My three kids, if three.

What is the best piece of advice you were ever given?
I very often regret personal decisions made under the influence of others. I prefer learning from my own mistakes.

What would people be surprised to know about you?
That I recently sang at a concert in Oslo Spektrum for 6,000 people?

If you could change one thing in the chess world, what would it be?
Stop agreed draws. That's match-fixing and cheating and not OK.

Is a knowledge of chess useful in everyday life?
Many have asked me if my chess-playing influenced my soccer, but I can't really see any relevant connections, neither to soccer nor to life in general.

What is the best thing that was ever said about chess?
Johann Hjartarson recently said: 'Chess is a hard job, but a good hobby'.